A Bite-Sized Public Affai

CW00404491

Do They Mean Us?

The Foreign Correspondents' View of Brexit

Edited by
John Mair and Neil Fowler

Published by Bite-Sized Books Ltd 2019

Bite-Sized Books Ltd Cleeve Croft, Cleeve Road, Goring RG8 9BJ UK
information@bite-sizedbooks.com
Registered in the UK. Company Registration No: 9395379

Bite-Sized Books Ltd Cleeve Croft, Cleeve Road, Goring RG8 9BJ UK
information@bite-sizedbooks.com
Registered in the UK. Company Registration No: 9395379
ISBN: 9781793477361

Acknowledgments

These books are always acorns that become oak trees through team enterprise. The book was John Mair's idea, the title derived from a BBC television programme three decades ago. Paul Davies was the midwife of the publication.

Alex De Ruyter of the Centre for Brexit Studies at Birmingham City University lent us his name and much more. Deborah Bonetti of the Foreign Press Association gave us her mailing list and support. Neil Fowler provided quick, professional sub-editing and Dean Stockton (as ever) a brilliant cover.

Mostly, though, our thanks go to authors who produced great copy – for free! – in record time. They are the heroes and heroines of this project.

John Mair, Oxford

Neil Fowler, Northumberland

The Editors

John Mair has taught journalism at the Universities of Coventry, Kent, Northampton, Brunel, Edinburgh Napier, Guyana and the Communication University of China. He has edited 26 'hackademic' volumes over the last eight years on subjects ranging from trust in television, the health of investigative journalism, reporting the 'Arab Spring', to three volumes on the Leveson Inquiry. John also created the Coventry Conversations, which attracted 350 media movers and shakers to Coventry University; the podcasts of those have been downloaded six million times worldwide. Since then, he has launched the Northampton Chronicles, Media Mondays at Napier and most recently the Harrow Conversations at Westminster University. In a previous life, he was an award-winning producer/director for the BBC, ITV and Channel 4, and a secondary school teacher.

Neil Fowler has been in journalism since graduation, starting life as trainee reporter on the Leicester Mercury. He went on to edit four regional dailies, including The Journal in the north east of England and The Western Mail in Wales. He was then publisher of The Toronto Sun in Canada before returning to the UK to edit Which? magazine. In 2010/11 he was the Guardian Research Fellow at Oxford University's Nuffield College where he investigated the decline and future of regional and local newspapers in the UK. From then until 2016 he helped organise the college's prestigious David Butler media and politics seminars. He remains an Associate Member of Nuffield. As well as being an occasional contributor to trade magazines he now acts as an adviser to organisations on their management and their external and internal communications and media policies and strategies.

Contents

It isn't personal, it's politics

In leaving the European Union the UK found a different way to become like the rest of Europe, says Deborah Bonetti, as the country's political stage began to resemble the chaotic states of many of its fellow European states. And the UK isn't the only member to be out of love with the institution

Europeans used to be in awe of Great Britain. The mother of all democracies, the biggest 'melting pot' in Europe, a champion of tolerance, respect, organisation and democracy. Politics in Westminster was considered a calm and civilised affair compared to the general feeling of chaos, particularly in my own country, Italy. For many of us, born within the EU timeframe, having Britain as a founding partner and driving force of the Union somehow gave it increased credibility and added strength to a project many of us passionately believed in.

Then 2016 came and Great Britain's long unease about the EU was laid bare for all to see. A referendum, considered madness by most other member states, had been promised and duly delivered. And the British turned out in substantial numbers – 72 per cent, as high a turnout as any other UK-wide vote in this country's recent history – to speak their minds.

Did the people of Great Britain like the EU? That was really the question. And the answer – after months of lies and ill-conceived predictions, shouted campaigns, broken electoral rules, populist anger at unregulated immigration, ignorance at what the EU had done for this country and many other divisive issues – was a resounding no. The Brits – or at least 52 per cent of them – did not like the EU one bit. They'd had enough, they wanted out.

From that initial moment of shock (I was so convinced this would not happen that I tried to place a bet on Remain, thankfully without success) the UK was plunged into chaos, which ironically made it look much more in sync – for once – with most other politically-chaotic EU states.

I remember reporting for my Italian daily newspaper, *Il Giorno*, in those first few febrile days after the vote, which stretched into weeks and months of relentless work. We all felt betrayed and the gist of most of the foreign press's articles revolved around the concept of 'Britain the treacherous'. The backlash from the rest of the EU could only be brutal.

As in any divorce, the jilted partner never feels too charitably towards the jilter. Anger, recriminations, accusations of betrayal were so rife, even in this country, that I know of couples who have split and friends who no longer speak to each other because they voted differently – or simply held opposite views.

On Facebook, some of my own friends back home asked me how I could suffer to stay in such a hateful country, why wasn't I going back immediately, how would I survive on solely British food once all imports of 'decent provisions' from the EU were stopped...

The fact that the EU never really was the land of milk and honey evoked by disgruntled Remainers was completely forgotten. Day after day my colleagues and I, here at the Foreign Press Association in London, came up with new stories as to how these Brits never 'got us', how they had succumbed to the lies of the Nigel Farages and the Boris Johnsons of this world, how they were always 'with a foot out' anyway: no Schengen, no euro, the 'special concessions or else' attitude.

And this, incredibly, hasn't really stopped, even two and a half years down the line. There still seems to be practically no other topic of conversation whether I speak with friends, colleagues, acquaintances or people I've just met in the queue at the supermarket. The country is furiously divided and each half still lashes out at the other. It seems there will never be another calm dinner party, unless the topic is specifically excluded.

And yet, while we all await to see what Brexit actually means, I have found it absorbing and exciting to be reporting in these hugely significant historic times, when Britain has (finally?) forgotten its stiff upper lip and has, ironically, become much more 'Italian'.

Theresa May and her cabinet of rotating ministers have evidently given up on that most British and revered virtue: 'calm'. Parliament and all political parties are entangled in daily wranglings, infightings, back-stabbings and betrayals, in flagrant disrespect of the mantra we all have on our mugs: "Keep calm and carry on". Britain seems to have finally Europeanised itself in leaving the EU.

What happens next is anyone's guess but did any of this feel personal? As soon as I say I am Italian (although I do now hold dual nationality) people queue up to apologise, or to reassure me that the vote was 'not against Italians, of course'. It was for 'many other reasons' (if they voted Leave) or it was 'an ignorant and irresponsible bit of the country' that voted like that (if they voted Remain).

Having been in this country for a quarter of a century, having studied here and having many wonderful British friends, I understand that the reasons for that vote were often complicated, visceral, personal and in many cases absolute. I have found that you can't really change the mind of a Leaver just as you can't that of a Remainer. And it is far too simplistic to label one good and one bad.

That is probably why the question was far too complex to be put to the people in such a simple way: in or out. Nobody ever explained what 'out' meant – as it turns out there are a plethora of possible 'outs', all of them not quite as good as staying in (especially in terms of the economy).

The single market, the customs union, the backstop and many other 'new terms' have entered the daily vocabulary of normal people, but behind them are hugely intricate processes. It is difficult to imagine that a second referendum could help unpack all these layers of complexity, in case the people were to be asked again. And what would the new question be? Without mentioning that the very principle of democracy, so central to this whole debate, would be at stake.

But whatever the outcome, the EU is obviously on tenterhooks and this helps to explain the rigid stance from Brussels: if Britain were to make a decent Brexit (not a success of it, even survival would do) who's to say other countries won't start queuing up to get the same deal? Two years after that fateful referendum, the UK is no longer the only country who has fallen out of love with the EU. This whole process has shaken the whole European project to its core.

About the contributor

Deborah Bonetti is Director of the Foreign Press Association (FPA) in London. She started working for an Italian radio station while studying for her first degree in English at UCL. She then freelanced for various news outlets and became deputy football correspondent for *Gazzetta dello Sport* (a leading sports daily newspaper in Italy). After getting married, gaining an MA and having a child, she moved on to *Il Giorno*, a daily Italian broadsheet (now compact), covering mainly politics and culture as its UK correspondent. She was President of the FPA from 2016 to 2018 before becoming its Director.

Section One: Over Here

Emotions across the spectrum

John Mair

This book is essentially the views of those charged with reporting Britain to the world – the Foreign correspondents in the UK. They are 'outsiders-insiders' – usually outwith the political process yet drawn, inexorably, towards the flame of reporting the British Brexit to their readers and viewers back home. They are the lens through which the world sees this moment of history/madness (you decide!).

First off, what do the correspondents from the EU (or near EU) countries make of it all?

Diane Zimmermann is the London correspondent for the German broadcaster ZDF and has had a very uncomfortable experience trying to explain Brexit to her German family and friends over their Christmas dinner table. They were perplexed – so is she and plain angry at the decision and the treatment she and other 'foreign' correspondents now get in Britain. 'Do they really mean us?' she asks, plaintively. They do!

Angela Antetomaso is also a broadcast journalist – for Italian TV – based in London. Post the Referendum in 2016 her new 'outsider' status was firmly brought home on the top deck of a famed London red bus in Westminster. Her verbal assailant was direct: "Get the f*** out of this country, you are not welcome here", was his message.

Bettina Schultz from Germany's *Die Welt* is, in essence, German British. She has lived here for a quarter of a century yet is still bemused by Brexit. She reasons that, sadly, the idea of Europe was always outside the imagination of the British. They simply never got it.

Tristan de Bourbon-Parme is the UK correspondent for no less than four newspapers in Belgium, France and Switzerland. He saw Brexit coming, despite the contrary wishes of his news-desks but he reads it as the people vs the elite in Britain.

His colleague Paola De Carolis from the Italian broadsheet *Corriera della Sera* goes back to basics and asks just what it means to be British today and what are the much-lauded British values post Referendum? In the uncertainty about the future she has applied for British citizenship.

Tonje Iversen is not an EU national but from Norway in the EAA – the supposed nirvana for those trying to avoid a hard Brexit. She was back home in Tromsø on 23 June 2016 with some local politicians. They were sceptical about Britons taking this leap in dark. They were badly wrong like so many of their British contemporaries.

Catherine Lough is a wannabe foreign reporter. She is among the more than 100 taking the prestigious MA in International Journalism at City University in London. I set her the task of going to Boston in Lincolnshire to see how the 'temporary Brits' – Eastern European migrant agricultural workers – view their future post Brexit. In a great piece of on-the-spot journalism she finds there is fear.

Jessica Buxbaum is another correspondent manqué at City University. She shows how the British press was (and is) in effect the Brexit Press – opinionated, biased and anti-European. In her view, the European press is much more objective on the matter. The British people are led by their papers – just two and a half of the 12 national dailies are firmly anti-Brexit. So, the Remain/Leave divisions in British society are magnified in print, though not in broadcast.

Finally, a bit of light relief among the gloom. Tessa Szyszkowitz of the Austrian news magazine *profil* felt so much for her British neighbours as they voted to exit the EU that she set up #hugabrit – which is what it says on the hashtag!

So, the entire gamut of emotions from love to hate through bemusement and more, those are the lenses of those at the ringside of the British Brexit It makes for fascinating reading.

Chapter 1

Variations on this one topic

**As a European foreign correspondent in a Britain facing leaving the EU, Diana Zimmermann more and more finds herself wondering: Do they mean us? Here she aims to understand what it's all really about.
Translated by Elizabeth Moseley**

Do they mean us? The title of this book is a great choice as it perfectly expresses the alienation, disbelief and bafflement currently being felt by a large part of the British public. I know the title of the book refers to Brits who do not recognise themselves in how they are presented by foreign correspondents.

But because the Brexit discussion is primarily about how the Brits feel, whether they have been betrayed by Theresa May, electively blackmailed, humiliated, lied to, deceived or at least disappointed or confused by the EU. I will attempt here to hold a mirror to my own position. As a German, and as a political correspondent in Brexit Britain, I increasingly find myself asking the question: Do they mean us?

Variation 1: The cringe factor

As I write in early 2019 I have just experienced quite a shocking trip to Germany to celebrate Christmas. Of course, on such a trip you inevitably meet up with good old friends and your dear family and talk on how the past year has been. But before I could even open my mouth, to tell them about the amazing new V&A gallery in Dundee, or the Abortion Referendum in Ireland or my trip to Blackpool, I was faced with knowing expressions of sympathy: "You poor thing," they said. But somehow, I had the feeling they were referring to themselves. "That awful Brexit, it must all be so boring for you".

Did they mean me? Or themselves, I thought. Well, yes, maybe it is a bit boring actually. I do now and then struggle to find an angle to the whole story that hasn't yet been explored. But it is also very exciting to be a foreign correspondent in a country at such a historically meaningful point in time. And there has been so much work to do I haven't really been bored over the past year at all.

"My mind starts going around in circles as soon as I hear the word 'Brexit' now", a friend said to me. "Will it ever end?" asked a relative, in the same tone he just used to address his screaming three- year-old.

The frustrating thing is that the Germans I met with over those few weeks are all completely fed up with the tedious details of Brexit. "Can't you just report on it once they have made their minds up?" was one common and well-meaning suggestion.

No, I cannot, I snapped. I found it very difficult not to take it personally. You spend years trying to explain the trials and tribulations of the island to the German viewer and all you get in return is the suggestion to just not bother. Instead of finding examples, carrying out interviews, presenting stories of immigrants, migrants and emigrants, fearful employers, hopeful Brexit opponents, scheming party members, I could have just spent the whole time using the same Asterix quote: "These Brits are crazy!"

If this book is with some bewilderment asking: "*Do they mean us?*" and by that mean the Brits, I ask myself does the German audience mean me? Or even more so: *Do they mean us*, the correspondents?

I am after all not the only journalist trying to explain the tribulations of Brexit. On the other hand, why should the Germans be interested in the finer details when they are clearly also alien to the ministers in charge of negotiating it?

A good example is Dominic Raab, who took until 2018 to recognise the importance of the trade between Calais and Dover. Or the Northern Ireland secretary Karen Bradley, who realised <u>after</u> being appointed that the issue of the unionists and nationalists might be a lot more complicated than she had anticipated. It also took an extremely long time until Liam Fox finally understood the issue of bilateral trade agreements.

The feeling of disaffection that so many Brits are experiencing with regard to the Brexit discussion, the uncomfortable impression that everything that is happening has very little to do with them, is something we correspondents, the messengers of madness, share with the British victims of Brexit.

Variation 2: Hope as a principle of perception

It is indeed very complicated. Take the backstop. We have tried to explain it on so many occasions, using graphics, words, examples, stories. Then I go to Germany to find that still very few understand it. The internal Tory Party vote of no confidence in Theresa May didn't make much sense to a German audience either. And when it comes to helping them understand why the British public still wants out of the EU when it is quite obviously a bad idea, this really shows the limits of media power.

Do they listen to us? Did we really do such a terrible job of explaining it all to them? You have to ask yourself when yet another person says: "I get the impression the Brits will come back". *Do they mean us?* Are they referring to anything we have reported? Can journalists create a certain impression without meaning to? Or is it rather that when a story doesn't make sense, reason kicks in and constructs a better one?

The complicated thing about Brexit is that it goes against general rules of storytelling. A good story has a beginning, a climax, and an end and follows the rules of logic or at least those of narrative art. Brexit has an unsuccessful beginning – a referendum that shouldn't have happened in the first place – a climax, that for almost half of the population felt like rock bottom, and a process, which flouts all patterns of logic.

We are trapped in a meaningless loop where politics and those reporting on it are desperately trying to keep up, while the issues that actually matter – those which led to Brexit in the first place – fall by the wayside amongst the madness.

But what's the alternative? Supporting Jeremy Corbyn, who when considering the biggest crisis in the country deflects attention by persistently reporting on the concerns of individual citizens? Rightly so. But he still fails to accept that Brexit is a result of the failure of the British political class to deal with large scale social hardship. When faced with the topic of Brexit he regularly plays the "Do they mean me?" card.

Variation 3: Identity crisis

One method of trying to dispel increasing confusion about whether this country is still the Great Britain we know, is to deal with the root cause. How can it be that the British ended up in such disagreement about the framework that should be used to organise their economic and political life, while almost every other European state seems to be much more relaxed about it?

What is going on in Britain when on the morning of 30 December 2018 *The Times* is stating: "A people who within living memory governed quarter of the world's land area and a fifth of its population is surely capable of governing itself without the help of Brussels." Really? Do they mean themselves? They don't even seem able to keep Westminster under control.

And conversely, *Do they mean us* when they talk about Europe? Really? As a super state that wants to turn the UK into a 'vassal state' and to keep this proud nation in a customs union against its will? Or, as Jeremy Hunt put it at the Conservative Party Conference, something resembling the Soviet Union?

The Brexiteers celebrated their 'Independence Day' on the night of the Referendum. In the same way they still do today in India and Nigeria, to mark their liberation from Britain? The longer Brexit goes on the larger the discrepancy between self-image and external perception seems to become. On both sides of the channel.

For a report on the British search for its identity via Brexit, I recently interviewed Gurminder Bhambra. As professor for Colonial History at the University of Sussex, she argues that Great Britain has experienced a kind of amnesia with regard to its colonial past. Most of the British public simply has no idea about the historical facts. There is a widespread, vague, rose-tinted view of the country's imperial past.

Bhambra is herself a grandchild of immigrants from India and has only ever had a British passport. For her parents, Great Britain has been their only home. Despite this, after the Referendum, she had to deal with people asking her why she was still there when they voted 'leave'. "For many people, it just wasn't clear that 'leave' meant Britain is leaving the EU, not that people like you and I should leave the country." *'Do they mean us?'* is a question she can answer unequivocally.

Variation 4: Unwelcome

There is the distinct impression that the British government would not only like to get rid of immigrants but would also be happy to see the back of foreign journalists. Foreign journalists working in the UK are largely ignored, and significant politicians very rarely agree to talk to us. The only time we are able to question them is if we manage to catch them on Abingdon Green in the five minutes they are bored waiting to move from a BBC interview to one for ITN.

Success in requesting interviews with ministers or even the Prime Minister is either unlikely or hopeless. Every few weeks there is a briefing at DexEU. Sometimes we see the caterers putting out teacups for the British correspondents (who are received separately from us). In Berlin (by way of comparison) the *Bundespressekonferenz* meets three times a week which both members of the national and accredited international press are invited to, regardless of the country they represent.

Not so in 'Global Britain'. Here all they seem to manage is to roll out five representatives from Downing Street, the Foreign Office and DexEU to receive questions from dozens of foreign correspondents without releasing any useful information in return. Even the press conferences at the Beijing Foreign Office during my time as a correspondent in China were more fruitful than they are here, though both events are similar in their apparent desire to keep us from our work.

The 'highlight' of the DexEU briefings for me was in the summer, when we asked in the simplest terms, which date Trump was due to visit the UK and were told once again we wouldn't be given any information about that, they didn't know etc. Minutes after leaving the building and its extremely poor mobile phone reception, people were practically shouting from the rooftops that Trump was scheduled to visit on July 13, confirmed by Downing Street. Had they not just briefed us? *Did they mean us?* Foreigners don't get any tea either, by the way.

Variation 5: Outlook

Should they stay or should they go? In the coming year there will be a lot of talk about coming and going. Will the Brits stay for a while and leave later? Or will they stay completely? Will they go for a while and then come back again? But if they don't go and do stay, that still doesn't mean that they really want to be an EU member.

The consequence of the Brexit result made us Europeans rub our eyes with amazement and on hearing what British voices were saying about the EU we had to ask ourselves: *Do they mean us?* Undemocratic, bureaucratic, unimaginative, supercilious, incapable of reform? That is certainly an area in need of some more self-reflection, particularly in Germany.

If Britain does now stay in the EU, it will of course not be because it suddenly thinks the Europeans are wonderfully creative and democratic after all. It will be an expression of complete resignation.

If Britain stays it will be because it is sick of arguing, because of poor preparation and the ridiculous political dramas and disputes in parliament that Brexit has caused. It will be because of the immense cost and the economic reality which no one anticipated.

Increasing numbers of Brits want to stay and I would wish it for them. But would it really be a good thing? Economically, yes. But politically it would be dangerous. It would lay bare the bankruptcy of British politics over the past few years and would create more space in the political arena for those on the right of the spectrum. And for the EU it would be a double-edged sword.

The European Court has ruled that Brussels has to open the door if London comes knocking. The resounding message from Brussels is still that most EU politicians would rather Great Britain didn't leave the Union. Is that really the case? Is the Union really in such bad shape? Can the already delayed reforms of a structure which is sometimes extremely slow to react in uncertain times really cope with yet another brake pad to hold it back?

What on earth will become of it if all the members of the club start doing whatever they feel like on the spur of the moment, if Britain were to return? "Hi there, we just needed a break to think about our relationship. But we are back now, for the moment at least". For as long as it takes until the right gather forces at home and until those left frustrated three years after winning a referendum and having been denied the result, decide they want to leave again.

The European Court may not have decided for this, but if it were possible, I would advise the EU to ignore the knock on the door with which the British might ask for the revocation of Article 50. Like: Do the mean us? No, thank you very much. We have other problems to solve.

Conclusion

If in the coming weeks the editorial departments from ZDF call and ask for reports on Brexit, my first impulse will be to ask myself: Do they mean us? Do they really want every detail? Do they expect our audience to listen to every twist and turn in British politics? Or should we just report everything once it's all over? Whenever that may be.

About the contributor

Diana Zimmermann was born in 1971 in Frankfurt/Main and is the ZDF correspondent for the UK and Ireland. She studied comparative literature, sinology and history in Berlin, Paris and Kunming. She was a reporter for ARTE in Strasbourg and Berlin and a correspondent for ARD in Beijing. She worked as the East Asia correspondent for ZDF from 2007-2011 and headed ZDF's foreign affairs magazine *auslandsjournal* before moving to London in 2015.

Chapter 2

The great divide

It happened on a bus, on a cold November morning. That was when reality hit Angela Antetomaso. The great divide between Britain and Europe was now real, and she was stuck in the middle

I would have never believed it could happen. Not to me. Not in the UK.

In all truth, the last few days before the Referendum, talking to colleagues and friends here and there, I could sense a great discomfort all around. I knew some of them were going to vote to leave the EU, even if they'd never admit it. It didn't matter, I kept on repeating to myself: after all, it was only a few of them. Brexit would never happen

And then it did.

That night, while the first significant results started coming out, when the unthinkable was slowly becoming reality, I was stunned. I knew my life would change for ever.

And it did.

It was only a matter of weeks before I ended up being the target of someone's rage, racism and frustration.

The bus to the City

It happened on a bus, one cold morning in November 2018. I was going to work, happily planning the day ahead. Being a television presenter, I was smartly dressed and made up, going through my notes and preparing for my live show.

On its way from Chelsea to the City, the bus was nearing Parliament Square when an elderly man nicely approached me. He smiled, said good morning and asked me where I was from.

I didn't see it coming.

As soon as I uttered the word Italy, his attitude suddenly changed: a long string of insults and abuse came out of his mouth, leaving me – and the crowd on the bus – totally shocked.

"Get the f*** out of this country, what are you doing here? Go back home, you are not welcome!"

Wait – was he really talking to me? I was frozen.

The entire crowd of commuters was looking in awe, but nobody uttered a word or raised an arm to stop him.

I got out of the bus as if in trance. I couldn't even react to that. I was speechless. Did THAT really happen? Did it happen to ME? I looked smart and business-like, I was happily minding my own business. How could that be?

Not a Londoner

In my mind, the images of my life in London started unravelling. I had been living and working here for about 20 years, this was MY home now. Did he really say I wasn't welcome – in my own home?

And that was when it really hit me hard.

I had always proudly seen myself as a Londoner. After the Referendum, I expected there could be some kind of divide, but not directly impacting my life. I was a Londoner, I had been here for so long...but only then I realised: for them I was not a Londoner, I was Italian. I was on the other side.

I was European – and by default, 'not welcome'. I didn't belong any more. It didn't matter that I had a (great) job, nor that I already had a job when I came here.

I had moved from New York to London because I was offered a position as a television presenter in the City, at Bloomberg Television. After a few years I had joined CNBC: ever since, I had been working as a presenter for its Italian-speaking channel.

Not only I had a job, but from the very beginning I had done all it was necessary to fit in. I arrived here in the late '90s: I landed in the UK on a Sunday afternoon and a few hours later, on the Monday morning, I was at work. The first day in the job my new employer did everything possible to make sure I could properly begin my new life in the UK. Before my training even started, they helped me open a bank account, set up my National Insurance number, sort out the formalities to help me rent a flat.

Since then, I had been steadily working every single day, and done all I could to settle in. I paid taxes, I registered with a GP, I had bought a house, a car, I had friends.

London was not only my dream – it was my home, and it had been for a very long time. I had a life here. I was settled. At least, I was – until now. All of a sudden, I started wondering if my future was really going to be here.

My world had changed

After the incident on the bus, things had changed inside me. I started noticing details I had never seen before: the way people looked at me, how they would sometime sneer or act dismissively...was it just my impression or was it real?

In all honesty, most of the time it was very real. It was all around me. Some people now felt entitled to take out their anger and direct it at foreigners, because that was the 'will of the people'. Truth is, it didn't even matter anymore if it was real or not: my whole world had changed anyway. I had changed inside.

The joy I always felt going to work every day, either walking through the streets of London or riding a bus across town to reach the office; the excitement of living in such a vibrant, wonderful city. All of that slowly began to fade.

My husband and I started talking about moving – but where to? This was home. Shall we go to Italy, or shall we explore other countries in Europe? There are so many beautiful European cities where we could easily settle and work...why stay here?

We started imagining our life out of the UK.

On the one hand, it was unthinkable to leave after so long – but on the other hand, would I still want to stay? That was my dilemma: after so many years working and paying taxes in the UK, I could easily request settled status or apply for British citizenship. The latter had actually always been in my mind, having spent most of my adult life in this country and totally loving it.

Was that still the case, though? Would I still want to be part of it, or was Theresa May's 'hostile environment' working on me as well?

Friends, colleagues, acquaintances...all of them kept on repeating how all that was happening had nothing to do with 'people like me'. I had 'such a glamorous job'; made 'good money'; was 'living the great life'...the hostility was only directed at the so-called 'low-skilled people'; the ones coming here with nothing and asking for benefits, the ones who came to 'steal jobs' and to 'take advantage of the free NHS'. That hostility was definitely not directed at the 'high-flyer' TV presenter – who, moreover, being a foreign correspondent, was by default not stealing anyone's job...

...but was that really true?

Would the British people be able to tell the difference between who came here to work hard and contribute to society, and who came to exploit the system? Would they even care to try to spot the difference?

I knew many people would. After all, this is a country that's always been the epitome of fairness and of perfect multicultural integration.

Tension grows

The problem, though, is that the hostile environment really exists – and often the hostility is palpable, and indistinctly directed at anyone who is not British – low-skilled and high-skilled people, low-income and high-income people...no difference at all. And that obviously includes people who, like me, came FOR work and who stayed TO work. People who made their life here.

Has anything changed since that incident on the bus? I have my doubts. As a foreign correspondent, I have been reporting about Brexit almost daily and I know the ins and outs of it all. And what I see from my point of view is that the divide and the tension are actually growing, not only between Britain and Europe but also amongst British people...and, in my opinion, all of this discontent is cynically being exploited by politicians in order to advance their career, by selling people the dream of independence and sovereignty – with the only result to make them poorer.

Making sense

I hope in the long run sense would prevail, but I don't think I will ever forget how much this country has changed after the Referendum. Truth is, I am only one of millions of Europeans feeling incredulity and disconcert about what we are seeing around us, and about our sudden fall into the 'unwelcome' category.

Such a striking contrast to the way I have felt for a very long time. When I first arrived, I had fallen in love with London, and London had embraced me with open arms. Over the years, I have always stayed so enthusiastic and happy, and believed my life was going to be here forever.

Do I still believe that now? I'm not sure anymore. Only time will tell, and luckily my job could take me anywhere. But one thing I do know: life in the UK, as it was before, will never come back. Nor for me, nor for anybody else – British and Europeans alike.

About the contributor

Angela Antetomaso is a television anchor and host, public speaker and moderator. She started her career in New York at CNN International and then moved to Bloomberg Television in London. After a few years, she joined CNBC as a presenter and a correspondent for its Italian-speaking channel. Angela has been daily hosting several live shows with in-depth interviews to high-profile guests including heads of state, CEOs and Members of Parliament. Over the years Angela has also regularly contributed, with daily financial news and commentaries, to various international TV Channels: CNBC Worldwide, Sky, Mediaset. She is a member of the board of directors of the MSc in Management at Cass Business School, City University of London.

Chapter 3

Did the British ever understand Europe?

'Europe' was always outside the imagination of the British – but it wasn't their fault, argues Bettina Schultz

Brexit is a mistake, a failed promise to the British People. I am sad about Brexit – but not surprised about it, not anymore. Brexit was inevitable after years of missed opportunities by successive UK governments, to understand what the EU is about und to explain this to the British people. The EU is so much more than just trade, regulating the labelling of fertilizers and sorting out the costs of roaming. Just look at the history.

My hometown in Germany is Osnabrück, former headquarters of the British Army in North Germany. I am a child of the cold war. At home I got used to British tanks on our streets 'to protect us from the Russians', we were told as children. When walking home from school, the sound of British fighter jets crashing through the sound barrier was a sign of summer and good weather.

The fear of war was real. I remember one day when my father suddenly told us over lunch: "If something happens and we cannot communicate anymore, each of us has to try to find his way to France, to our holiday home in the South. We will then meet there." It was clear what he meant. He did not want to experience another war. He had been in the Second World War as a child soldier at 15 years old. His own father eventually died because of his injuries and illnesses, after he had been shot in France in the First World War at the age of just 17.

Early lessons

I learned at school what horrific consequences a dictatorship can have and how vital democracy and power sharing is. Germany had to start from scratch after its dark history. For us, the EU was always a success story of the willingness of all member states to work, trade and live peacefully together.

Most member states of the EU are constantly making a new effort, every day, to find compromises, to adhere to common rules, to have this block of friendly nations growing together to stop the danger of conflict, hate and war. The scars of the two world wars – and the Cold War – are too deep. This willingness to stick together is the foundation of the EU. It is why the British Government failed in dividing the opinion of the EU member states when negotiating Brexit.

Meet the British?

Throughout my 25 years in Britain I have always felt that for the majority of the British people the political meaning of the EU is pretty irrelevant. There is even a certain arrogance when I am told that the UK does not need a peace project. The UK was a peaceful nation anyway and a better democracy too. Britain easily sheds the responsibility for its mistakes (Iraq, Libya), rejects the refugees of its wars with an audible sigh: 'So good we are an island'.

I have reported from the UK as an economic and financial correspondent for more than 25 years. During this time sentiment towards Brussels was often ignorant, sometimes even hostile, stirred up not only by most of the British press, but also by successive UK governments.

Norman Lamont lamented that the UK crashing out of the European Exchange Rate Mechanism (ERM) was the mistake of the German Bundesbank. John Major stirred the sentiment against the EU with his 'non-cooperation-policy' because of mad-cow disease – Bovine Spongiform Encephalopathy (BSE). The British people are told that the EU is 'undemocratic' (it is not), a bunch of too many countries that never can agree on anything sensible (it was the UK who insisted on ever more member states coming into the EU) and that 'Brussels is inventing irrelevant and burdensome regulations' (not true) without any say of the UK (never mind the powerful influence of the British in Brussels).

I have never experienced a UK government even trying to explain some of the thousands of EU laws and regulations that make trade and life in the EU across borders easier than anywhere else in the world.

EU as the scapegoat?

After years of failed domestic economic politics, the UK Government uses the EU as a cheap scapegoat for the failings of successive governments. Only the EU has nothing to do with it.

For many years the UK has suffered from a lack of funding and investment in schools, vocational training of the young, apprenticeships and state-funded universities (the £9.000+ fees per year are an insult to British young people and prevents social mobility at an early age).

The systematic lack of productivity in UK manufacturing, the lack of infrastructure in the country, lack of funding of local authorities bleeding from many years of austerity and the lack of funding of the NHS have nothing to do with the EU. The lack of proper long-term economic policies for the neglected North of England, the outright poverty of socially weak people, the lack of funding of care for the elderly and the low pensions are the mistakes of the short-term policies of successive British governments and not the EU.

Short termism

Not enough is done with a long-term view. This undermines the economy and leaves a growing part of the population frustrated. But instead of tackling these failings with a redirection of policies, more investment, more long-term sustainable policies, British politics turned on Brussels and EU migrants as scapegoats and targets. More moderate voices were drowned, pushed aside, which was the most shocking experience of all my years here in Britain.

When I moved to London in 1991, I was impressed by the openness of British society, by the ease of how all cultures and religions could peacefully and successfully live and work together. But my impression was superficial. I was deeply worried when I experienced how quickly Brexit shattered this innocent coexistence. Suddenly British politicians chose to pick Brussels and EU migrants as scapegoat for their own failed politics. They were convenient targets of course, as neither Brussels, nor EU migrants, could vote in the referendum.

Suddenly questions were asked that I thought belonged to the ugly past. Where do you come from? How long have you been here? Do you just want 'our' benefits? Do you just exploit 'our' NHS? Are you undercutting our wages? Suddenly we were not welcome anymore.

I have lived in this country more than 25 years. I have paid UK tax during these years, never accepting a penny of benefits. I have private health insurance; I sent my girls to private schools; employed my nanny legally. I dutifully filled out dozens of pages, provided documents and paid fees to get British passports, just to be on the safe side. All the while listening to Nigel Farage ranting about immigrants.

What Britain gains from the EU

Too many people believed in the populism of Farage, of Boris Johnson, of David Davis, of Michel Gove, and of Jacob Rees-Mogg. They told the British people that their life will be better outside the EU and enough people did vote for Brexit, but they had no clue about the difference between the EU, the Single Market, the Customs Union, the European Economic Area, Schengen and the Monetary Union (EMU).

The UK does not need to leave the EU to export and trade successfully, to get Free Trade Agreements (the EU has more than 50), to get its borders back (the UK is not in Schengen), to be able to devalue the pound (not being in the EMU). The UK does not need to fear the European Court of Justice (no other country has so many cases decided in favour of its position).

On the contrary membership of the EU allowed the City of London to grow as the powerful gateway to the financial markets of Europe; membership of the EU fuelled inward investment in manufacturing as a bridge into European markets; being a member of the EU gave Britain a powerful seat at the table whenever anything was negotiated and decided by Brussels.

And immigration? In 2004, the Blair government opened the UK labour market for 10 new EU countries even before the UK was forced to do so. And the 'vast' amount of money the UK pays to Brussels (remember the rebate) is a tiny fraction of the whole budget. And still, during more than two years of negotiations with Brussels the UK Government was at pains **not** to explain anything of this to the British public.

Behind the scenes, in the small print of negotiations, the UK Government tries to secure as much of the EU market access as possible, swallowing EU regulations as a future rule taker. Look at the technical papers about preparations for a 'no deal'. It is a list of dozens of regulations the UK Government will adhere to just to prevent serious economic damage.

Will Brexit succeed?

Brexit will be a failure. Of course, the UK will make its way outside the EU – no doubt about it. Brussels and the UK will replicate enough of the small print in a free-trade agreement to succeed economically. But it will be a failure for the British people. The British public will eventually realise that Brexit will not change their life a bit and it will not help with all the failures of domestic politics. But the scars of Brexit will go deep – for a generation to come.

About the author

Bettina is a freelance who writes about economics and politics for *Die Zeit* and other magazines. Her journalistic career started after studying microeconomics and finance when she joined *Frankfurter Allgemeine Zeitung (FAZ),* a German weekly. In 1991 she moved to London as the foreign financial correspondent for *FAZ,* leaving 25 years later to freelance. She wrote a book about her experiences of adopting from India – '*Namasté my daughters*'. Bettina likes creating ancestry books for families setting their experiences into historical context.

Chapter 4

A rational vote against a rational argument?

Tristan de Bourbon-Parme sensed the Leave vote approaching, but never thought it meant him. Here he tells why he saw it as a social stand against the political and economic system shaped over the last 40 years

It is 6.30am on Friday 24 June 2016, and my phone rings much earlier than usual. At the other end of the line is the editor of the international section of *La Libre Belgique*. "You did warn us, but we hoped that the final count would lean towards the other side", he said, in a voice betraying a sense of vertigo as he imagined the possible consequences of the result of the vote.

For some weeks I had told them that the Referendum could only result in a vote in support of Brexit. My certainty was based on what the politicians omitted to say for most of the campaign; a month before the vote, the Leave camp hadn't yet raised the topic of immigration, which had guided then Prime Minister David Cameron's decision to hold the Referendum in the first place. Still, the polls predicted 53 per cent in favour of remaining. This seemed to me a very narrow margin that would be easily swayed.

I had not, however, shared my wavering sense of confidence that Brexit would go ahead since the murder of Labour MP Jo Cox a week before. Some supporters of Brexit with whom I had previously spoken made the effort of contacting me again to tell me that they had changed their minds, and that they would vote to remain so as not to be associated with her killing.

For what seemed like a moment, I thought this group might be representative of a larger movement in changing voting patterns, and maybe it was – I now assume that without this monstrous act, the number of voters choosing to leave would have been much more substantial.

Leaving what?

In the months preceding the Referendum, I travelled across the country for my articles, and met nobody who liked the EU and thought that remaining would be a good idea. Apart from a handful of rare exceptions of former or aspiring Erasmus students, from Romford to Glasgow, via Dover, most of my interviewees usually expressed a wish to leave the EU, though often with a tinge of self-doubt, as one stated: "I want to leave the EU, but will I be brave enough to vote to leave?"

None, it seemed to me, were rejecting this European organisation in and of itself; neither Remainers nor Leavers know the ins and outs of the organisation well enough to vote on it. For the latter, the EU represented the status quo touted by David Cameron, and the political and economic reality their country has known for the last 40 years. To reject it meant to reject a system that had turned them into second-class citizens.

It's true that few of them would probably describe their decision in these terms, though I would argue not because they don't believe it. Rather, I think there is a watered-down rhetoric in local politics and the media, a general avoidance of loaded conceptual terms such as (de)centralisation, capitalism, and socialism, absent from everyday discourse. Aside from 'sovereignty', a persistent term in British political debates, most political ideas are expressed within tangible systems – welfare is relegated to the NHS, care happens in the community, and risks are the stuff of banking.

During the Referendum campaign, discourse pivoted on control, lost and (re)gained. 'Control' had the power to extract the country from the jurisdiction of the European Court of Justice. 'Control' could put an end to the competition posed by European migrants for access to employment, social housing and places in day-care centres or schools, and the wage stagnation generated by their arrival in lower skilled jobs. 'Control' could hold politicians accountable, as Labour had been until the 1990s. Lastly, 'control' would expose the social injustices of economic growth benefiting only metropolitan centres, while peripheral cities, villages and neighbourhoods suffered from impoverishment.

It was not so much the Referendum campaign that led me to believe that a Leave vote was imminent, but the research I had done since coming to the UK in 2009. I had witnessed the effects of neoliberal policy across the country, in neighbourhoods and peripheral post-industrial cities like Huyton, Fleetwood and Wythenshawe, where public services have been shrinking, where privatisation has favoured the dereliction of infrastructure, particularly transport, and where decentralisation has left local authorities to themselves.

Contempt and sore losers

At 7am on 24th June, I went out to interview locals about the outcome of the Referendum. I approached a group of workmen before they began their work, as they gathered under scaffolding and were each enjoying a mug of warm milk tea. When I stopped to ask what they thought of the results, they hesitated and glanced at one another, no doubt reluctant to entre a discussion with a Frenchman. Clearly suspicious, they did not divulge much.

As I continued to stand about with them, one asked me what I thought of the result, and I briefly replied that I was not surprised and understood the motivations of the majority vote. I felt a mix of astonishment and relief on their part, as if they had been prepared to be rebuffed and judged by my answer. They slowly opened up, and the conversation grew into a highly personal and rational discussion. I felt like it must have been the first time that a journalist listened to their concerns, their fears and their hopes and that someone of a different social class, university educated and well-travelled, showed an interest in their opinions without judgment.

The workmen were not the only ones to be suspicious of people from other social milieu, as the prism of social class continues to shape perceptions in the United Kingdom. Suspicion is therefore a sentiment widely shared among the British upper classes and upper middle class, most of whom are either Remainers or 'lost sovereignty' adepts? As I write, many have not accepted the legitimacy of the Leave vote and do not perceive it as a social stand against the status quo. Some reveal themselves as sore losers, expressing contempt for this popular vote and for the voters themselves, calling them 'stupid' and arguing that "they did not know why they voted to leave".

However, everyone I met who had voted for Brexit did so consciously and with serious reflection, weighing the negatives against their far-reaching visions and hope.

One of the workmen had said, "I voted to leave the EU for my children, for future generations". Another admitted that "there may be a slight economic drop-out but it will not last. The zombies are not going to invade the country, the sky is not going to fall on our head as the Remainers had threatened. There will be enough work here for people to get by". Or a third: "We will be able to preserve our public services, our welfare state. This is for me the most important. And it will probably not be easy in the beginning, we will have to adapt to this unknown that comes before us, but the country will not collapse. We are solid, we will hold up." Their votes may have been desperate, but they were also optimistic.

The scale of the significance of the vote

The Referendum was the single most profound democratic exercise the British people have known in their lifetime. It was a unique opportunity to voice their opinion on their living conditions, and to shift politics directly. Therefore, the rational arguments put forward by political and economic leaders during the campaign did not engage with the majority's life experiences: anyone who had never profited (or considered themselves as having profited), from the growth experienced during the Blair years, cannot be afraid to see it collapse, and rather perceives this as a chance for change. To renege on the implementation of the Referendum is to reject the scale of its significance and silence an entire population.

Even in the London borough of Islington, where I have lived since 2010 in an ex-council flat, all my neighbours voted to leave. In my eight years here, I have made friends in the block and rarely felt that my ever-obvious French accent and European-ness has set me apart or ever brought about any animosity.

I have never asked myself the question "do they mean us?", and I don't think they mean me (except for a minority of xenophobes): I do not compete with them for essential public services as a worker and taxpayer, so I do not fit into the categories accused of weakening the country. None of that has changed since 23 June 2016.

About the contributor

Tristan de Bourbon-Parme moved to London in December 2009. He is the foreign correspondent in the UK and Republic of Ireland for the national dailies *La Libre Belgique* (Belgium), *La Tribune de Genève* and *24 Heures* (Switzerland), *La Croix* and *L'Opinion* (France). After beginning his career in Paris at *L'Humanité,* he was correspondent for the French press in Sydney, Seoul and Beijing. He is the co-author of *La Corée dévoilée – 15 portraits pour comprendre* (2004), Paris, L'Harmattan.

Chapter 5

Citizens of somewhere or citizens of nowhere?

What does it mean to be British and what are so-called British values? Paola De Carolis poses the questions

"I don't mean people like you," the taxi driver said as the lights of a wet London night streaked past the window. "You're fine. You're not really an immigrant".

When I arrived in London in the mid-1980s, I was one of a handful of non-British students at my school. My otherness made me exotic. Did I really leave Italy for the UK? Did my grandmother make pasta by hand? How had I managed to learn English? I was praised for my accent and questioned about the weather. I have now lived in the UK for more than 30 years, but I began to feel properly foreign in the run-up to the Referendum.

The hostility towards immigrants took me aback. 'Cockroaches' (*The Sun*, 17 April 2015), 'Violent thugs and rapists clogging up the prisons' (the *Daily Mail*, 3 June 2015), invaders, pests, leeches sucking the blood out of the NHS, social provisions, the job market. Whatever ends up happening with Brexit, it's the language on immigration that for me was the biggest disappointment.

Initially, the Referendum was disheartening because it crystallised the lack of belief in a world order that had, amongst other things, made my existence possible. I had relished the ability to travel and settle where I wanted without paying too much attention to geographical borders. If I could attend university – at the time there were no fees – and apply for jobs in this country, it was because of the EU.

The economic forecast for a post-Brexit Britain were dire, but would it really be that bad? A divorce, after all, doesn't have to be ugly. A deal would be found, Britain would leave the EU in an orderly fashion and the new situation would become normality. I hung on to optimism, until it was no longer possible.

The exploitation of immigration

I was as surprised by the right-wing exploitation of the concept of the evil immigrant as I was by the inability of the moderates to counterbalance it. Brexit didn't need to be all about immigration, yet the idea that there was stream of foreigners coming to the UK 'usurping' housing, services and jobs and that leaving the European Union was the way to stop it took hold.

I listened in disbelief as sensible, balanced, educated friends said they would vote Leave because the NHS was at breaking point, their children couldn't get jobs and teachers and nurses couldn't afford to live in London.

My feeling is that the UK knows little of the raw, hungry, desperate immigration it's so frightened of. It has no experience of boats docking daily on its shores with hundreds of refugees in need of immediate medical attention. This is a world-wide, humanitarian emergency that no-one should feel entitled to wash its hands of, not Theresa May's Britain and not Matteo Salvini's Italy, but it doesn't involve the UK in the way it involves the countries that form the frontiers of Europe.

What Britain gets from the EU is mainly immigration deluxe. Young graduates that are keen to work hard and make the most of the opportunities that a meritocratic society offers; students that at some point will provide valuable intellectual property – doctors, nurses, engineers, builders, architects, artists, musicians.

They are net contributors to the British economy. European immigrants pay more in tax than they take in services. That is the case not only overall, but also in as far as the NHS is concerned. In fact, according to Oxford Economics, European migrants each pay £2,300 more a year to the Exchequer than the average British citizen. Are these the people the UK won't want quite so much in the future?

The Referendum was not about facts and figures. The contribution of EU nationals to the UK was not given the same coverage as other aspects of immigration. When, in December 2018, the Migration Advisory Committee spelt the numbers out again, they were treated by many newspapers as if they were new, while they were not. It's a pity that the country was not given the fuller picture. It could have led to a more constructive debate about the sort of future it wanted.

Why I love the UK

It has been difficult to watch Brexit unfold because if I, like many other European migrants, am here, it's because I love this country. It's not an abstract affection. I love the sense of fairness I perceive, I like that you can appeal parking tickets, that you can call the council to check your neighbour's extension doesn't break the rules, that the parks are immaculate, that the streets are clean, that there are playgrounds everywhere.

Equally, I love that those playgrounds are filled with children of all colours and backgrounds, I love that my children at school mark Diwali, Eid and Hanukkah as well as Christmas, that many of their friends are British but are also from somewhere else. I love the inclusivity and the respect for others, the ethnic and cultural diversity of British writers, the self-deprecating sense of humour.

I've admired and liked the orderly work of parliament, the two-party system, the fact that in moments of crisis the country pulls together. Brexit inevitably has changed some of this. Is inclusivity real? How can it coexist with mistrust of foreigners? Is multiculturalism truly valued? As a foreigner I feel there's something un-British about the divisive political machinations surrounding the deal.

"I am foreign". "You don't sound it", said the taxi driver. "What are you going to do about it?"

After all these years, I have now applied for British citizenship. The Government keeps saying Europeans living in the UK are welcome. "We want you to stay". How true is this? From March 2019 we will be able to apply for settled status. It will be straightforward and cheaper than the current procedure for residence, we are told, but what rights will it grant us?

Will Europeans settled in the UK always have the same access to the labour market? Will we always be taxed the same way as British citizens? Will we continue to be able to own property? What happens if we go and live somewhere else for a few years? Will we still retain settled status in Britain? In the uncertainty I opted for British citizenship. At the same time many British friends are applying for European nationality through a spouse, a parent or a grandparent. It feels like a game of Passport Monopoly.

What makes you British? What makes you foreign? What's British about so-called British values? Do they not belong to the whole of humanity? Acquiring a second citizenship is not an emotionally straightforward transaction.

"If you believe you are a citizen of the world, you are a citizen of nowhere," said Theresa May in March 2018. "You don't understand what citizenship mean." I don't agree. I am more in line with Adam Smith, who in *Theory of Moral Sentiments* in the 18th century wrote: "He is not a citizen who is not disposed to respect the laws and to obey the civil magistrate; and he is certainly not a good citizen who does not wish to promote, by every means in his power, the welfare of the whole society of his fellow-citizens". By this definition, I have been a citizen of the UK for a very long time. Most of us foreigners have.

About the contributor

Paola De Carolis writes for Italian broadsheet *Corriere della Sera*. She arrived in the UK with her parents in 1984. When her parents returned to Italy three years later, she stayed in Britain to finish her education. She has three children and a dog and enjoys walking daily in various parks in North London.

Chapter 6

Strangers on the shore?

After the EU Referendum the town of Boston on England's east coast became famous for its high proportion of Brexit voters. Now the Eastern European community there is fearful for its future, as Catherine Lough reports.

When I meet Martyn Chambers, deacon at St Mary's Catholic Church in Boston, Lincolnshire, he describes the town as 'geographically isolated'. Mike Cooper, a Conservative councillor, suggests that many Westminster politicians could not place Boston, or Lincolnshire, on a map.

Boston is a picturesque market town, dominated by the medieval tower of St Botolph's Church, known locally as the Stump. In 2001, its population comprised just 55,750 people, 97 per cent of whom were White British (ONS, 2001). By 2011, the population had grown to 64,637 people, 15.1 per cent of whom were immigrants.[1]

As people migrated from Eastern Europe to work in local farms and factories, Cooper suggests the demographic shift was a 'massive, seismic change'. He cites this as the reason behind the 2016 EU Referendum result. This 'isolated' place had the highest recorded percentage of Leave voters in the country, with 75.6 per cent voting for Brexit (BBC, 2016). For the national media, Boston was suddenly on the map.[2]

Why Brexit?

Local politicians give various reasons for Boston's support of Brexit. Anton Dani, an Independent councillor who formerly represented Ukip, blames the pace of change. "If you suddenly have an influx of 30,000 people,

people start to resent that", he says. Anton seems an unlikely Ukip candidate; he is Moroccan-born, and his wife is Polish. Indeed, we discuss our families' experiences of immigration – Anton moved to the UK in the 1980s, working briefly for Marco Pierre White;' my father emigrated from Argentina at the same time'. Now, he runs *Café de Paris,* a European-style deli in Bridge Street. Yet he criticises the lack of integration in Boston as a factor behind the result.

Boston is rural and labour-hungry, so there can be no suggestion that migrants are competing with locals for jobs. Mike Cooper says the town has "always relied on overseas labour" but cites pressures on infrastructure and housing as a reason for the result. Unscrupulous landlords exploited the increasing demand: "We've found some absolute horror stories. People living in sheds two storeys up. That's why people said, *Enough is enough"*, he says.

Cooper acknowledges the Government's austerity measures may have exacerbated problems. Boston is a low-wage economy, and Boston Borough Council lacks the funding to build new homes (Boston is also on a flood plain, which makes it expensive to build). One of the local estates has no money for street lighting at night. "Then they say austerity doesn't hurt people". Has it made him doubt his own party? "Yes".

Not everyone agrees that immigration levels have been excessive. The agricultural economy relies heavily on migrant labour. Sue Lamb, who manages Lamb's Flowers in nearby Spalding, says that of the 50 people she employs, there is one British person – a supervisor. "And that isn't that we don't look for local people, they just simply aren't there. Without [immigrants] we're scuppered".

Complex issues simplified

She feels people voted for Brexit "partially out of ignorance" yet were also misled by the Leave campaign. In her view, it simplified complex issues: "The thing with a referendum is, it's one question that really covers a hundred, or a thousand questions. But we are desperate for these people. The way we've treated them and made them feel will be to our cost".

"People don't realise how they actually fill the plate. How when you go to hospital, nine times out of ten, it's not a migrant who's taken your place, it's a migrant looking after you".

Her words are borne out by research from the Migration Advisory Committee (MAC, 2018) which found that EU migrants contributed £4.7bn more in taxation than they received in benefits in 2016-17, as well as contributing "much more to the health service [...] than they consume".[3]

The report does echo concerns in Boston about pressures on housing. Immigration can increase rental prices through greater demand, yet the report suggests that, rather than being a net result of migration, these issues are partly caused by political decision-making, and local authorities with 'a higher refusal rate on major developments'. Arguably, pressures on services are caused by a lack of planning and foresight from the UK Government.

How does the Polish community feel?

For the Polish community, the Referendum result has caused considerable uncertainty. Outside St Mary's Church, I speak to Eva Kowalska, an administration worker who moved from Poland in 2006. She describes Boston then, when it was 'a small village'; now, its streets are bustling. "Eastern Europeans built Boston, basically," she says. "Ninety-nine per cent of the people in the fields and the factories were Polish".

After Brexit, she feels she can no longer plan for the future. She is unconvinced by Theresa May's wavering assurances that EU migrants will be protected; the lack of clarity is too unsettling. "A lot of Eastern Europeans are terrified". She describes friends who have paid into mortgages, fearing they will return to Poland with nothing. "I think I will leave. I had a lot of dreams here [...] But [Theresa May] hasn't decided, and even if she does, she won't tell us the truth".

Eva had thought of Boston as her home, but she feels uncomfortable now. "I don't want to feel like a stranger here". Her experiences with locals have been positive, and she was shocked by the Referendum result. She feels people were swayed by promises of improvements to the NHS. "Maybe they thought there would be less [immigrants], but they didn't know what they were doing. I think they should have a second vote".

Przemek Frankowski, who works in the White Hart Hotel, also supports the idea of a second referendum: "I've always been pro-EU – I feel it's better to be within something bigger than being separate". He has lived here for 13 years and has never felt unwelcome in Boston ("I've blended within the

British community") but thinks the impact on services might have contributed to the result, as well as drunkenness from a minority of immigrants.

Przemek has not witnessed visible tension or racism, although he does recall hearing people say "We want our country back" when television crews visited the town in 2016. For Przemek, who has a young daughter, what concerns him most is uncertainty over the future of EU migrants in the UK.

"That's the one thing I would get worried about. We hope we're not going to be told, 'Oh, well, I'm sorry but you have to go. We don't want you anymore.' That wouldn't be fair on anybody".

Miki Bura, a fellow employee who moved to Boston aged nine, says his parents felt shocked and unwelcome after the Referendum. "People around here thought we were really coming to take over, but that's not true. All we're trying to do is get a fair play in life".

Newly-arrived immigrants are understandably more nervous. Zlana and Zlatiana Goneva, who moved from Bulgaria in 2017, run a brightly painted café selling crepes and pastries. Zlana was stunned by the result. "We came here to live our whole life. When you hear people voted against us, it means they don't like us. It's strange, because we don't make problems. We work, we help their economy".

A misrepresented place

At St. Mary's, I speak to Martyn Chambers as Father Kowalski prepares for the Polish-language mass. Throughout our conversation, parishioners arrive bearing parcels for a Ukrainian children's charity. When children sing in Polish at the front of the mass, the sense of belonging is palpable. It seems absurd that anyone would question the Polish community's presence here.

Martyn feels Boston is misrepresented as a fractured or divided place. "We had easily in excess of 20 nationalities at the English morning mass. Polish people attend the English mass. To make out the Polish community has been a problem ignores the other communities we've had for many, many years". He points out the long-standing Keralan, Filipino and Portuguese communities here.

For Martyn, people voted for Brexit because they were misled, especially with regard to promises about the NHS. "Politicians were throwing out facts and figures like confetti". Boston's size and geographical isolation may also have led to resentment over rising immigration levels. "The difficulty for Bostonians was the speed of change".

Despite this, he thinks "there is a great sense of community. If you go into schools, the children all have friends of different nationalities". Indeed, the Ofsted report for Staniland Academy, which has a high proportion of EAL (English as an Additional Language) students, describes pupils who are "curious about each other's cultures and backgrounds, and get on noticeably well together".[4]

"The changes are coming through the young people of the town," says Martyn. "And I passionately believe that's showing already".

Notes

1. Based on data from Lincolnshire County Council's *Lincolnshire Research Observatory Report on Country of Birth, Ethnicity and Nationality of Lincolnshire Residents*.
2. Articles about the Brexit vote in Boston have appeared in *The Guardian, The New Statesman, The Financial Times* and *The Irish Times* since the EU Referendum.
3. MAC (2018) *Migration Advisory Committee Report: EEA migration in the UK* p.3 and p.73
4. Office for Standards in Education (2013) *School Report for Staniland Academy* p.6

References

Office for National Statistics (2001) Available online at http://www.research-lincs.org.uk/UI/Documents/2001%20Census%20Lincolnshire%20and%20Districts.pdf/ Accessed on 30 November 2018.

Lincolnshire Research Observatory Report on Country of Birth, Ethnicity and Nationality of Lincolnshire Residents (2011) Available online at http://www.research-lincs.org.uk/UI/Documents/country-of-birth-ethnicity-and-nationality-of-lincolnshire-residents-census2011-112013.pdf/ Accessed 10 December 2018.

BBC News (2016) Available online at https://www.bbc.co.uk/news/uk-politics-eu-referendum-36616740/ Accessed on 30 November 2018.

MAC (2018) Migration Advisory Committee (MAC) Report: EEA migration in the UK: Final Report. Available online at https://www.gov.uk/government/publications/migration-advisory-committee-mac-report-eea-migration/ Accessed on 10 December 2018.

Office for Standards in Education (2013) School Report for Staniland Academy. Available online at https://reports.ofsted.gov.uk/provider/21/138752/ Accessed on 8 December 2018.

About the contributor

Catherine Lough is a freelance journalist studying for the MA in International Journalism at City, University of London. She previously worked as a secondary English teacher in inner-city London and Barcelona. She has an MA in Education and International Development from the Institute of Education and has worked in a voluntary capacity for Amnesty International UK and Amnesty Chile. Her research interests include education, development studies and human rights. She can be contacted by email at Catherine.lough@cantab.net.

Chapter 7

A new identity, a new enemy

Tonje Iversen remembers exactly where she was the day the UK voted to leave the EU – in a bar in her home town of Tromsø with three Norwegian politicians, one from the Conservative party and two from the Socialist party. None of them thought Brexit would happen; Brits are just too conservative and it's way too dramatic to leave the EU were the main arguments that night. How wrong they were

Brexit was a massive surprise in Norway. A few months after the vote I moved to London to work as a reporter for two Norwegian news outlets. Brexit was going to dominate in the world of foreign affairs for quite some time.

Of course, I was expecting people to have opinions about Brexit and to feel strongly about it, but I was not expecting it to be as divisive as it has been. People I have known as very calm and composed, clearly showed their outrage in social media. Sometimes in a brutal way, especially when they wrote about Leavers.

Brexit was personal. A new identity was created. Either you were a Leaver or a Remainer. And depending on which box you ticked you became friend or enemy.

Brexit appeared to be the painful heartbreak you never get over. A heartache followed by denial, followed by rage and resentment. Followed by ideas about how the UK could get back together with its long-term partner again. The impossible break up, a love story coming to an end.

At least for many people – but for many others this was liberation. Freedom from what many see as an elitist undemocratic organisation. An abusive relationship that had to end. A partner you do not really understand and that seems anything but fair or transparent. To them the Remainers became the enemy, the 'out of touch' elitists who would like to overthrow the will of the people. The losers of the Referendum who dared to accuse and label them as stupid, ignorant and racist.

It became clear that people did not 'have' opinions about Brexit, they had 'become' them. Thus, every conversation about Brexit became personal. Every attack on the side you adhered to became as if you where the one being attacked, not a view or an opinion, but your very self. And so, everything you attached to your identity, every value you had were under attack.

It was as if Brexit has become the free zone where everything is allowed. Where everyone is entitled to say whatever they want without having to listen. The topic where it is legitimate to be abusive, in particular in social media.

The soft compromise

Before June 2016 Brits used to ask me about the Northern Lights, Norwegian politics and the suicide rate in Scandinavia. Now it's Brexit. What do I as a Norwegian journalist in the UK think about Brexit? What do I think about being a member of the EEA, how do I feel about a soft Brexit modeled on Norway, or a Norway + model?

I do not feel strongly about Brexit. And I always sense disappointment that I'm not outraged enough. If Norway had been a member of the EU I might have felt it more personal. Like the UK was leaving me too. Or rejected me. Rejected the country I'm from.

Norway voted twice to stay out of the EU. Something that earned us a place on the map as 'the greedy selfish fisherman's land'. But Norway is strongly tied to the EU through Efta and the EEA.

We may not be a part of the customs union, and not a member of the EU, but we adhere to all the rules and laws of the single market. I could move freely to the UK, as I did for the first time in 2010 to study. I remember I was annoyed to find out that I had to pay much more in tuition fees than my European friends as a consequence of not being from an EU country.

The majority of politicians in Norway talk of EEA as a good compromise. Many politicians would rather see Norway as a member of the union, but as the people voted to stay out, EEA is seen as the best solution.

However, my impression is that most people would like to either be in the EU or out, not half way in as many people see the EEA. It is not seen as a great compromise because the people who are pro EU think it is ridiculous to pay money and adhere to all the rules without having a say. The people who do not like the EU argue their case pretty much in the same way and some feel that the Norwegian parliament and the political elite snuck Norway in through the back door.

Making a mess

The UK was probably more shocked than any other country the night of 23 June 2016. I know my news feeds surely were. In particular my British friends expressed their shock and surprise. The look on British politicians' faces was pretty revealing too. This did not go as expected. They were not prepared, and it became clear, pretty soon, that this would not be the easiest thing in the world.

A British journalist asked me to describe Brexit with just one word, but I now rather describe it with three – divisive, turbulent and messy. After Brexit, British politics has been dominated by questions without any solid answers, uncertainty, chaos, U-turns, indecisiveness, opportunism, in-house fighting and confusion.

My Conservative friend called me a few weeks after I moved back to London in 2016 and said: "Brexit is never going to happen. I might have been wrong about the vote but it is a too complex task, it is simply impossible". Now, more than two years after he still reminds me: "Look at the mess in Westminster, I told you so, it will never happen".

About the contributor

Tonje Iversen is a journalist from Northern Norway based in London. She mainly contributes to TV 2, Norway's biggest commercial broadcaster, providing live analysis pieces, comments and reports on current affairs, politics and society in the United Kingdom. She has a Master's degree in political journalism from City, University of London and a Bachelor's degree in broadcast journalism from Gimlekollen in Kristiansand.

Chapter 8

How the British and European press framed Brexit

Jessica Buxbaum believes an analysis of European and British press coverage of Brexit shows that European media is mostly objective in its reporting while British journalists' highly partisan framing of Brexit news is deepening the political divide in the United Kingdom

To first understand how the European and British press covered the Brexit Referendum and subsequent aftermath, a general knowledge of the differences and similarities of their news sectors is necessary.

While at least one tabloid dominates circulation in nearly every European country, a broadsheet is part of the top three widely-read newspapers in many nations such as Germany, Spain, Austria and France. The same is not true for the UK where the three most read newspapers – *The Sun*, the *Daily Mail* and *the Daily Mirror* – are all tabloids.

Britain's fixation with tabloids stems from the country's regard for social stratification. Class is engrained into the cultural framework of British society and Britons take discernible pride in their class identity, not just in their work but also in the news they absorb. While broadsheets and broadcasters are typically consumed by the middle to upper class, tabloids are meant for the working class. And with 60 per cent of the Britons identifying as working class, it remains no wonder why tabloids are popular.

Historically, both the European and UK media are overwhelmingly partisan compared to their United States counterparts. While Britain, like the US subscribes to the Anglo-Saxon media system – where journalists are considered objective watchdogs – the British press still exhibits a high degree of partisanship in its reporting.[1]

Comparatively, British media is more right-wing than Europe. Media tycoon Rupert Murdoch owns both *The Sun,* a traditional tabloid and *The Times*, tabloid in shape but broadsheet in nature. Right-wing ideology dominates British news, outnumbering leftist thinking from the *Daily Mirror*, *The Guardian* and *The Independent*. Thereby, sensationalist tabloids hold considerable political clout and sway over public opinion.

How the UK covered Brexit

Following the UK joining the European Economic Community in the 1970s, the press was increasingly Euro-enthusiastic. Yet in the 1980s the pro-Community stance of the media gradually reversed.

Stemming from the changes in political parties' positions over the UK's role in Europe, the resurgence of European federalists and heightened competitiveness of newspapers gave way to the development of a Eurosceptic press. In 1990, *The Sun* attacked former European Commission President Jacques Delors over suggesting a single currency with the headline 'Up yours Delors!'. This notorious report marked the first wave of bloated and shrill anti-EU coverage.

By the time of Brexit, British media was already an established Eurosceptic institution. The anti-EU sentiment of the press drowned out outlets advocating for Remain. A Reuters Institute for the Study of Journalism analysis found that in the run-up to the vote, 41 per cent of articles about the Referendum were pro-Brexit while 27 per cent were advocating to stay in the EU.

The UK's leading newspapers – *The Sun*, the *Daily Mail*, the *Daily Telegraph* and the *Daily Express* – disseminated a steady stream of anti-EU reporting. Examples included:

- On 6 February 2016, the *Daily Telegraph* published a story saying Abu Hamza's daughter-in-law "cannot be deported from Britain despite a criminal past because of human rights laws, an EU law chief has ruled".

However, a court ruling did not happen – this incident was merely an opinion from a European Court of Justice's Advocate General.

- On 16 May 2016, the *Daily Express* published the story 'Soaring cost of teaching migrant children'. detailing the cost of educating children from the EU had hit £3.2bn per year. This story was inaccurate because it defined anyone with at least one parent from the European Economic Area as a migrant child.
- On 15 June 2016 – just eight days before the fateful Brexit vote – the *Daily Mail* published a front-page story with the headline 'We're from Europe – let us in!' next to a picture of a lorry of migrants. The migrants were actually from Kuwait and Iraq.

Ipso required the newspapers publish corrections of these errors, but those were merely tiny acknowledgements, not nearly as prominent as the original stories.

Broadcast, on the other hand, was not much better. Broadcasters are subject to strict impartiality regulations, so the BBC rarely grilled its interviewees and turned its platform into a debate between the two sides. The BBC became obsessed with balance during this period as it was entrenched in negotiations with the government over the renewal of its ten-year charter. In the UK, newspapers dictate the news agenda and the BBC appeared to echo the hostile press rather than acting as a media leader.[2]

The Brexit campaign's main message was 'Take back control' and this sentiment was mirrored in the British media. Explosive language dominated news before and after the Brexit vote. A King's College London study found that campaign coverage was 'acrimonious and divisive'. Common words used in pro-Brexit reporting included 'fury', 'attack', 'slam', 'scaremongering' and 'Project Fear'. Fear-inducing language was used in the press coverage of both camps, illustrating catastrophic outcomes if Brexit did or did not happen.

"Rather than seek to provide a public space in which each side could fairly challenge the other, many news outlets encouraged and stoked the partisanship", the authors of the King's College London study wrote.

How Europe perceives Brexit

Compared to the shrill British press, European outlets took a calmer approach in covering Brexit. Europe sympathised with Britain but was also relatively unconcerned over Brexit's impact, according to a Reuters' Institute study. While opinion dominates British news, European media was predominantly fact-based and neutral. The Reuters analysis found that 82 per cent of European Brexit news did not take a position over Brexit, with only 18 per cent expressing their view. When opinion was taken, it leaned heavily against Brexit at 75 per cent.

Excluding Ireland – which had a significant stake in Brexit negotiations – European countries mostly reported from a UK perspective rather than from national interest, again showing a clear disengagement over Brexit's impact on the EU.

Sympathy still remains a defining characteristic of European coverage. When Theresa May negotiated a deal with the EU in November 2018 that was subsequently criticised by her colleagues, European newspapers sympathised with the Prime Minister.

"Rarely has a government leader taken so many punches, suffered so many humiliations and faced so many jibes and betrayals", French daily *Le Monde* 's editorial board wrote.

And Spanish newspaper *El Pais* said, "It's easy to criticise her, but no one else dared to oversee the titanic task of destroying the road the UK has been on for 45 years".

British versus European Brexit coverage

The economy was the most-covered issue in Brexit reporting by both the European and British press. Yet while the economy was more widely reported, immigration tripled over the campaign period in British news. Immigration stories consistently splashed over the front pages, with 99 covers dedicated to immigration and 82 focusing on the economy.

Not only did the number of articles on immigration spike, but the word count should be noted as well. Right before the vote, *Daily Mail* stories on immigration averaged 807.9 words, 19 per cent more than articles on the economy which averaged 699.3 words.

Over a third of Europe's Brexit coverage focused on negotiations. The rest centred on other issues, with the economy occupying nearly half of that reporting. Given the core of the EU is shared economic interest, articles relating to trade are unsurprising. However, more surprising was the little coverage immigration was given, just 10 per cent – a stark comparison to British journalists' fascination with the topic.

The lead-up to the Referendum and the initial shock of Brexit pushed European press to frame it in crisis terms with language like 'Earthquake in Europe'. This narrative, akin to a natural disaster, has died down in recent discourse. Yet the British media might have missed the memo to tone down the rhetoric as they remain tightly clutched to their explosive dialogue.

Opinionated, sensationalist headlines regularly appear like 'Brexit sabotage: Britain's former EU negotiator says Remainers can still stop Brexit' and 'Doctors ignore will of their patients with Brexit vote call'.

British media stoking the divide

'Enemies of the people' screamed the *Daily Mail* over judges who sided with a case against the Government over implementing Brexit without approval from Parliament. Papers on the left and right continue to stoke divisions over Brexit, increasingly switching their target from outside to inside Britain.

"The written press reflects the divisions in the country", radio host Iain Dale told the *Columbia Journalism Review*. "I think you'll find, in most of the country, that the shift in public opinion has not been great since the Referendum".

Brexit was supposed to heal political cleavages and unify, but it's only strengthened the divide. A UK for Changing Europe research found that after the Brexit vote, Britons remain polarised. And as newspapers continue to exacerbate the schisms with divisive coverage, the divide may foreseeably worsen.

Notes

1. Mancini, Paolo. (2006) 'Is There a European Model of Journalism?', in De Burgh, Hugo. (ed.) *Making Journalists*. London: Routledge, pp. 77-93.
2. https://foreignpolicy.com/2016/07/08/the-tragic-downfall-of-british-media-tabloids-brexit/

References

Allsop, Jon (2018) *Partisan voices are drowning out Britain's Brexit debate*, 10 January. Available online at https://www.cjr.org/analysis/brexit-the-sun-independent.php, accessed on 2 December 2018.

Barnett, Steven (2016) *The Tragic Downfall of British Media*, 8 July. Available online at https://foreignpolicy.com/2016/07/08/the-tragic-downfall-of-british-media-tabloids-brexit/, accessed on 1 December 2018.

Borchardt, Alexander, Simon, Felix M., Bironzo, Diego (2018) *Interested but not Engaged: How Europe's Media Cover Brexit.* Available at (Accessed: 25 November 2018).

Mancini, Paolo. (2006) 'Is There A European Model Of Journalism?', in De Burgh, Hugo. (ed.) *Making Journalists*. London: Routledge, pp. 77-93.

Centre for the Freedom of Media (2017) *Are British media failing the test of reporting Brexit?*1 March. Available online at http://www.cfom.org.uk/2017/03/01/are-british-media-failing-the-test-of-reporting-brexit/, accessed on 25 November 2018.

Daddow, Oliver (2016) *UK Newspapers and the EU Referendum: Brexit or Bremain?* Available online at https://www.referendumanalysis.eu/eu-referendum-analysis-2016/section-4/uk-newspapers-and-the-eu-referendum-brexit-or-bremain/, accessed on 25 November 2018.

Harding, Gareth (2017) *Media Lies and Brexit: A Double Hammer-Blow to Europe and Ethical Journalism.* Available online at https://ethicaljournalismnetwork.org/resources/publications/ethics-in-the-news/media-lies-and-brexit, accessed on 25 November 2018.

Mair, John, Clark, Tor, Fowler, Neil, Snoddy, Raymond and Tait, Richard (eds.) (2017) *Brexit, Trump and the Media,* Suffolk: Abramis.

Moore, Martin and Ramsay, Gordon (2017) *UK media coverage of the 2016 EU Referendum Campaign* Available at https://www.kcl.ac.uk/sspp/policy-institute/CMCP/UK-media-coverage-of-the-2016-EU-Referendum-campaign.pdf (Accessed: 25 November 2018).

Nugent, Ciara (2018) *'Sad.' 'Weak.' 'Anemic.' How Media Across Europe Described the U.K.'s Brexit Chaos,* 15 November. Available online at http://time.com/5455804/europe-media-brexit-deal-fallout/, accessed on 25 November 2018.

Payne, Rita (2018) *Brexit and the British Media* 31 January. Available online at https://www.commonwealthroundtable.co.uk/general/media/brexit-british-media/, accessed on 25 November 2018.

Ponsford, Dominic (2017) *The Express was a repeat offender when it came to misleading press coverage ahead of UK 's vote to leave the European Union,* 17 November. Available online at https://www.pressgazette.co.uk/fake-news-was-not-in-evidence-during-run-up-to-brexit-vote-but-misleading-news-published-by-biased-national-newspapers-was/, accessed on 25 November 2018.

Ridge-Newman, Anthony, León-Solís, Fernando, O'Donnell, Hugh (Eds.) (2018) *Reporting the Road to Brexit:* International Media and the EU Referendum 2016: Palgrave Macmillan.

Sogelola, Deborah (2018) *Brexit, Agenda Setting and Framing of Immigration in the Media: The Case of the Daily Mail, LSE Undergraduate Political Review,* Vol. 1, pp 128-142.

The UK in a Changing Europe (2018) *Brexit and public opinion* Available at http://ukandeu.ac.uk/wp-content/uploads/2018/01/Public-Opinion.pdf (Accessed: 2 December 2018).

Wilkes, George and Wring, Dominic (1998) *The British Press and European Integration* Baker, David and Seawright, David (eds.) *Britain For and Against Europe? British Politics and the Question of European Integration,* Oxford: Clarendon, pp.185-205.

About the contributor

Jessica Buxbaum is a freelance journalist currently pursuing a Master's degree in International Journalism at City, University of London. She previously worked as the Senior Editor for Carbonated.TV, a political news website representing 'The Voice of the Underdog'. Her main areas of focus are global politics and the Middle East. In addition, to Carbonated.TV, her work can be found at Joe.co.uk, Tikkun Magazine and Crosscut News. You can reach her on Twitter @jess_buxbaum.

Chapter 9

The flipside of Brextremism

Tessa Szyszkowitz believes journalists should get politically active sometimes. Here she explains why and what it meant for her to co-found #hugabrit.

The idea that Britain might leave the European Union had upset me since the idea of a Referendum was floated by Eurosceptics in the Tory party. To me it is a sign of civilisation if European leaders spend their time negotiating over the degree of how much a cucumber should be bent, rather than sending their armies against each other on the battlefields.

As an Austrian I was always convinced of the need for the EU. I know Britons do not necessarily feel that way. Unlike the countries on the European continent the United Kingdom has not been invaded for nine centuries. The prospect of peace and security on the European continent is not as ostensibly important to people here.

As I watched Euroscepticism rise and Brexit becoming a real option, I decided to forgo my usual journalistic impartiality and to become politically engaged. After the British General Election in May 2015 my friend and colleague Birgit Maass, the UK correspondent of *Deutsche Welle* said to me: "I think we should do something to prevent Britain from leaving the EU". I instantly agreed with her. Although it somewhat clashed with our belief in journalistic neutrality, we came to the conclusion that in matters of principle journalists should be allowed to take a stance, too.

No vote, so we spoke in public

As EU citizens in the UK we were not allowed to cast our vote in the Referendum. Our only chance to raise our voices was to speak out in public. Throughout the winter of 2015-16 we developed a grass roots movement from scratch. The making of #hugabrit and @pleasedontgouk became a fascinating case study for the creation of a social media campaign for us. And it changed our lives.

The tone needed to be strictly positive and the message so friendly that nobody could accuse us of being patronising. But we also needed to find something cheeky and controversial enough to get attention.

We wanted to use two of the characteristics Britons are famous for: their sense of humour and their reputation of being reserved, even averse, to personal contact with strangers. We also wanted to use the fact that all teenagers and socially conscious people take selfies all the time. We created a website www.pleasedontgouk.com, where we uploaded pictures of EU citizens hugging their favourite Brit, along with a few sentences about their story. Using the hashtag #hugabrit these images were linked to social media via Twitter, Instagram and Facebook accounts. The idea was so simple that everyone could participate.

For a while I hoped to call our campaign – which should be a love bomb to Britain – #LoveBlitz, referring to the name Britons gave the bombing campaign of Nazi Germany against British cities in 1940. I asked Timothy Garton Ash what he thought of it. I will never forget the bewildered look in his eyes. We dropped the idea. And opted for #hugabrit.

Most of our group members were of that opinion anyway. Marianna Rosenfeld, an Italian art restorer; Katie Lock, a German photographer; and Rosa McNamara, an Irish doctor were involved early on. The Swedish marketeer Amanda Ullman and the German social media expert Christine Ullmann came later. They brought Verena Enderle with them, a genius designer, who invented our logo. Paul Varga, an Austrian inventor, was the only man who enthusiastically threw himself into our pro-bono operation.

How the campaign took shape

In the winter months #hugabrit started to take shape. At the same time the official campaigns 'Vote Leave' and 'Stronger In' took off. Well-funded and oiled. David Cameron's Remain camp paid £9m for a booklet which was put in every letter slot in the country and bored people deeply. #hugabrit by contrast did not have a budget at all. When approached by pro-European groups, who offered to sponsor us, we declined. We wanted to stay strictly independent.

Instead, the launch party of #hugabrit received contributions from likeminded European wine shops and restaurants in London. Austrian Cafè *Kipferl*, Italian restaurant *Sardo, Scandinavian Kitchen* and *La Fromagerie* donated their specialities. We were by then overwhelmed by the support #hugabrit got from all over Europe and the UK. Many more people than expected came to the party. Two weeks before #hugabrit had gone viral on social media after Tim Dowling had written about us in *The Guardian* (http://www.theguardian.com/commentisfree/2016/apr/07/prepare-love-bombed-britain-hugabrit-jarvis-cocker?CMP=oth_b-aplnews_d-2). After this my phone never stopped vibrating.

From the middle of April onwards we had a flood of interview requests. I organised smaller hug-ins for TV teams, radio reporters and daily papers. We counted 140 articles and broadcasts at the beginning of June in *El Pais, Le Monde, Wall Street Journal, Die Welt* and on the BBC, CNN and ARD. Sometimes we had to put an article through Google Translate to figure out what language it was written in.

Eurosceptical British papers like *The Sun* or the *Daily Mail* accused #hugabrit to be 'un-British'. One columnist discussed how he would explain to his wife why he let a 'long-legged Italian beauty' hug him. #hugabrit could not help him with this dilemma. But for us every mentioning of @pleasedontgouk in the media was good. It led to more images being sent to social media with hugs from Cambridge, Thessaloniki or Brussels.

At a hug-in on Parliament Square, in front of Big Ben, a reporter from Barcelona TV asked me if our concept is not a little 'naïve' given the complexity of the matter. "The best things come out of an embrace", I answered.

A hug for Nigel Farage

By the way: I will dispute from now on that Britons don't like to get hugged. My first #hugabrit was with the English artist Jeremy Deller. The Turner Prize winner was bewildered but not against a hug. After all, he was absolutely for staying in the European Union. #hugabrit co-founder Birgit Maass even hugged Nigel Farage, the EU-phobic Ukip boss, live on BBC *Daily Politics* TV. He turned pink in her embrace in the most beautiful way – https://www.youtube.com/watch?v=gEZEgxCgn_U

And then Farage and his companions won. On 23TH June 2016 Britain voted to leave. Since then the debate has turned even more bitter and hate filled.

The longer the negotiations with Brussels have gone on, the more it became apparent how difficult it is to get out of a rather fruitful und constructive 45-year relationship. The lies of the Brexiteers have become apparent to many people who voted to leave. Even if Brexit will happen on March 29, it will not be a triumphant Iindependence day. Rather an inglorious exit of a member state with Britain still following most of the EU rules for years without having a say in it. Or jumping with no deal from a pretty high cliff into the unknown.

Brexit has created a deeply divided country. The forces of English nationalism are being let loose, archconservative backbenchers of the Tory party suddenly have huge influence in parliament. It will be hard to put these destructive ghosts of the past back into the box.

I know of many stories of EU citizens in the UK feeling unwelcome here today, though I must say that my own experience is very different.

First of all, I lived seven years in Putin's Russia before I came to the United Kingdom. I am used to – let's say – 'not belonging'. I make my home wherever I go, but I always stay a 'Luftwurzler'. My roots are in the air. I am not 'a citizen of nowhere', to quote the silly expression Theresa May coined two years ago in her poor attempt to become a populist. My Austrian passport protects me well from being stateless. But my European state of mind lets me live and think freely and believe that nationalism is not everybody's answer to the 21st century.

I have never had bad experiences myself and even arch-Europhobes like Bill Cash assured me: "This is not personal, this is not against you." But more than that. Our pro-European campaign #hugabrit meant not only that we EU citizens put our arms around British women and men. They also hugged us back. Our movement was only a drop in the ocean of Euroscepticism in this country, but it kept me emotionally afloat.

My British friends are deeply ashamed of their country turning its back to the European Union. Most of them are still fighting hard to prevent this from happening.

Brexit has not only set English nationalists free. There has never been so much pro-European energy in this country than now. As the political establishment is struggling to find a satisfying solution to the Brexit vote of 2016, civic engagement seems to be called for. Some 700.000 people came out on the streets of London from all over Britain to call for a second referendum on October 20TH[t] in 2018. Even if Brexit is still coming, the pro-European energy will fuel new political movements. This is the good news in this winter of Brextremism.

About the contributor

Journalist and historian Tessa Szyszkowitz is the UK correspondent of the Austrian news magazine *profil*. Formerly a Russia, Middle East and EU correspondent, she has lived in London since 2010. Her bilingual website is www.tessaszy.com. In September 2018 she published the book *Real Englishmen – Britain and Brexit* at Picus Verlag (in German).

Section Two: Over There

Confusion *sans frontieres*

Neil Fowler

If observing and understanding the Brexit debate has been tough for foreign correspondents actually based in the UK, consider the difficulty it has posed for those living and working on the European mainland itself. Whether infuriated by the result of the Referendum or showing some understanding of what had happened, the view from Europe itself was certainly mixed.

Philip Sime, based in Brussels, observes how he believes that city will be even more important to the UK after Brexit has happened.

"More than 40 years after it was first raised, the lowering of the Union Flag in the capital of Europe will see the UK walk away from the institutions which govern its largest trading partner. As a result, Brussels will become more, not less important for British diplomacy as London seeks to influence the EU after Brexit," Sime says.

Meanwhile Nathan Gallo sees amazement in France at the UK's decision to leave but also looks at how the Gilets Jaunes actions at the end of 2018 in France may have been influenced by the Brexit movement, noting similarities between the two countries where there have been significant declines in the image and reputation of the political classes on both sides of the English Channel.

"If each phenomenon had its national specificities, all of them showed one thing – that a large part of the citizenry was not willing to listen to traditional politicians and media anymore. All these events were the expression of a deep anger coming from people and areas that have been overlooked for years," Gallo writes.

Danish journalist Mette Rodgers asks the question: 'Who are the 'nutters' now?' in response to those who believe that Brexit was the start of a domino effect in Europe, with the Danes quickly following suit. Nothing is further from the truth, she says.

"On the contrary, the invitation from the Brexiteers to join the exodus have instead had the effect of reminding the Danes – and other Europeans – why we should be part of the EU, despite the parts of it which we do not like."

However, that view is not necessarily shared in some of the eastern nations of the EU where some of the core values of the EU are under close examination. Hanna Liubakova believes that Brexit could just be a sideshow with Poland and a potential Polexit, for example, becoming a more important threat to the union.

"The EU is not merely a union of trade and money; it is also a union of values. Those values – human and civil rights, freedom of speech and tolerance – are under threat. Defending them is crucial – and won't be a piece of cake,' she writes.

So, a diverse range of opinions from across the EU. There is no unified view of what it all means – except that the unknown unknowns, as former US Defence Secretary Donald Rumsfeld may have said, may well outnumber greatly the known knowns.

Chapter 10

The view from Brussels

Despite the Brexit regret felt in Brussels, the EU knew that in 2018 it had to drive a hard bargain with the UK if it were to survive. Britain, for its part, would come to view the so-called capital of Europe as an increasingly important diplomatic destination after Brexit, says Philip Sime

On a wintry night in January 1973, the Union Flag was raised in Brussels. Of course, the raising of this flag in a foreign land was not extraordinary. It had fluttered in the breezes of Britain's far-flung colonies for centuries. However, there was something new about this occasion. For the first time, the raising of the Union Flag represented the UK's joining of an economic union on course for rapid expansion into a fully-fledged political union.

In the UK, there was a growing realisation of Britain's downgrading from a superpower. The country, which had ruled the world's waves, now watched as its trade links shifted closer to home, the result of the 'winds of change' sweeping across the colonised world. For Britain, the writing was on the wall. Both in economic and diplomatic terms, its future lay in Europe.

However, the EEC had its own reservations about the UK's membership. France's Charles de Gaulle famously vetoed the UK's attempts to join the club. In words which seem remarkably prescient today, he warned that Britain has a 'deep-seated hostility' to the European project. Nevertheless, the *feu vert* was eventually given and the UK joined the EU.

In a telling sign of successive governments' suspicion towards European integration, London forged a unique path in Europe; mostly keeping the EU at arm's length. 'Cherry picking' and 'having your cake and eating it' are two phrases which we now associate with the Brexit negotiations. However, they are also expressions which encapsulated the UK's relationship with Europe from the 1970s onwards.

The UK secured several opt-outs, something which was possible due to it being a big fish in a small pond. "The UK won pretty much everything, always", said Alyn Smith, an MEP who by 2018 had represented Scotland in Brussels for 14 years. But things were about to change.

My Brexit story

With my suitcase and rucksack, I arrived in Brussels in the summer of 2015, just one of the many British students who, each year, throw themselves into the Erasmus programme. As a political obsessive, I found it unashamedly exciting to be at the centre of the action when the then British Prime Minister, David Cameron, began his regular commute to Brussels to further improve the UK's relationship with the EU.

At that time, there was pretty much no expectation that the UK would ever leave, something which was reflected in the deal with which Cameron returned to Westminster. Fast forward a few months to June 2016 and he was touring the UK on a mission to convince Brits to vote to remain in the EU. Meanwhile, Europe was waking up to the possibility of Brexit, a word which, by the way, was adapted from Grexit, the previous headache for Brussels.

For my part, I had moved onto the second stage of my Erasmus programme and was studying at a university in Valladolid, Spain. As the only student from the UK in my classes, I was nicknamed 'Británico' by the lecturer and quickly became the focus of a politically-engaged class's questions about Brexit.

"You could be our last British student!", it was once put to me by our concerned linguistics professor. I confidently laughed off the comment, predicting that the UK would stick with the status quo. As it turns out, my political antennae were proved to be about as accurate as those of our ill-fated former Prime Minister. However, despite that, I've since managed to achieve my goal since the age of 13 and am now working in international journalism based in – you guessed it – Brussels.

Britain in the Brussels bubble

Brussels is a city which has seen its fair share of political crises. However, all paled in comparison to the hammer blow that was the EU's second-biggest economy voting to leave the bloc.

However, it wasn't just about economic power. Recent history had proved the UK to be a vital ally. I spend much of my time at work either in the EU area of Brussels or in Strasbourg and am continually struck by the number of streets, quarters and even tram stops which carry the name of Winston Churchill.

But it didn't matter to whom one spoke in Brussels at the time, it was almost always seen as beyond doubt that the EU would be worse off without the UK. Britain, with its former superpower status, world-leading financial centre, impressive diplomatic network and its defence and intelligence infrastructure had given the EU power on the world stage.

However, the Brexit regret felt in Brussels failed to translate into much goodwill. If the EU was going to make it into its next decade, it couldn't fixate on the past.

The independent MEP and former Ukip leadership contender, Steven Woolfe, said the EU was 'angered' and 'bemused' at the Brexit decision. That's why there was a harsh acceptance of the decision to leave and a steely determination, much to the frustration of London, that the future UK-EU relationship would mark a break from the UK's tradition of having its cake and eating it.

Woolfe revealed that Britain's 'respected civil service' provoked concern in Brussels as Brexit talks got underway. "If anyone in the EU wanted to know what was happening in another country, they'd only need to go to UK civil servants", he said. However, whereas once the arrival of an RAF jet at Brussels Zaventem Airport would signal the imminent commencement of tough negotiations, it now proceeded what many saw as a farce. And it was Britain's political leaders who now elicited a combination of amusement and despair in the EU capital.

Brussels-based communications consultant and *British in Europe* representative, Laura Shields, believed the way in which the negotiations were conducted had damaged the UK's 'reputation for pragmatism, moderation and reliability'. "We've got a Rolls-Royce being driven by idiots", was how Alyn Smith characterised this juxtaposition of a well-respected civil service and what was seen as a chaotic political leadership.

For anyone who had been following the UK's negotiation with the EU, the photograph of the paperless former Brexit Secretary, David Davis, meeting with Michel Barnier, his EU counterpart, illustrated this perception. "Michel Barnier was there with his folder and his file. Davis is grinning like a half-wit on steroids, just glad to be in the room. And Barnier is looking like 'who's the chancer?'", said Alyn Smith.

It is important to remember that Davis insisted that this moment was, in fact, a set up by the Commission. However, like it or not, optics are a big factor in politics and that snapshot of their meeting in the Berlaymont building captured the new reputation of Britain in Brussels. However, it is also important to understand that the EU was yet to face its most challenging part of the Brexit process: the future trade negotiations. Indeed, Pieter Cleppe, the head of Open Europe's Brussels bureau predicted that trade talks would 'divide the EU' as the withdrawal negotiations had created divisions for the UK.

The Scottish perspective

It was a fascinating time to be British in Brussels. Of course, Brexit was far from the only important issue facing the EU, however, it continued to feature prominently among the talk of this town. According to Laura Shields, Brexit was viewed in Brussels as a 'soap opera'. Indeed, when meeting politicos and non-politicos alike, a sly grin often came over people's faces when they learned that you were from the UK. However, it was more often than not replaced with a broad smile when they further learned that you were originally from Scotland.

What now?

I hadn't expected it but there existed a strong recognition in Brussels that Scotland was significantly more pro-EU than its neighbours south of the border. It was a recognition those in favour of Scottish independence believed could prove vital in the coming years. SNP MEP Alyn Smith described a 'chill' which existed towards his party during the 2014 referendum on Scottish independence. However, it now seemed that Brexit had shifted the political sands in Brussels. Smith said that the UK's withdrawal from the EU had 'hugely inverted' the way many viewed Scottish independence in Brussels. While polls failed to show a groundswell of support for Scottish independence, it could not be denied that a pro-EU, independent Scotland could prove to be the victory that Brussels could snatch from the jaws of Brexit defeat.

More than 40 years after it was first raised, the lowering of the Union Flag in the capital of Europe will see the UK walk away from the institutions which govern its largest trading partner. As a result, Brussels will become more, not less important for British diplomacy as London seeks to influence the EU after Brexit. Despite what many might expect, the UK's exit from the EU will likely lead to a much-larger and more active British presence in Brussels.

About the contributor

Philip Sime is a producer on the *Raw Politics* programme at Euronews NBC. The programme is broadcast daily from the heart of the European Parliament in Brussels and Strasbourg and asks the critical questions that are defining and dividing society today. Philip previously studied a Master's degree in Broadcast Journalism at City, University of London and an undergraduate degree in French, Spanish and European Union Studies at the University of Edinburgh. You can follow and contact him on Twitter: @PhilipSime.

Chapter 11

The UK facing Brexit: 'La perfide Albion' lost in translation?

To French journalists, Brexit embodies how the United Kingdom has become a narrow-minded nation deluding itself about its role in the world, says Nathan Gallo. It has also stressed how UK politicians and media have overlooked a deep popular anger for years, hence reminding the French movement of the Gilets Jaunes

'Brexit, see you soon' – the headline of the French newspaper *Libération* on 26 November 2018 is voluntarily ironic and bitter. For the day before, Theresa May had eventually managed to come back from Brussels with a deal. But one month later, no one could tell what was going on. Coming back? Leaving for good? With what type of relationship with the EU?

The last months of 2018 showed the complete confusion and the fragile state of the political sphere in the UK. In French newsrooms, Brexit was seen as a big waste, like an unsuccessful and painful divorce.

Who's flying the plane?

'Afflicted', 'confusing', 'irrational politicians', 'auto-destructive political context': every time I talked to French journalists covering British politics, all of them admitted to being dismayed by the Brexit Referendum followings. "Each day confirms my feeling: no one is on board anymore to drive UK out of the Brexit turmoil", said Quentin Dickinson, chief of the European affairs of the public radio group Radio France.

Daniel Desesquelle, a radio producer for RFI, summed up the situation in two words: "On the one hand, *mediocrity* of UK politicians; on the other hand, *illusion*, in which the British population is living at the moment", he said.

On one side of the argument, the British politicians have failed to act as responsible actors. While Theresa May is admired for her resilience and her political engagement, French journalists were astonished to observe the violence and the weak level of the debates.

"The current political stage is really ignorant when we talk about juridical and technical knowledge", Quentin Dickinson said. But politicians were also accountable for the original mistake of the Referendum itself: "The question at the Referendum was insane", Sonia Stolper from *Libération* told me. "The question was too simplistic for an answer that is way more complex. The EU was used as an outlet by UK politicians".

Playing Astérix against the whole world – not a brilliant idea

But on the other side of the argument Brexit was not only about getting rid of the EU. It had also become a fantasy for a country willing to reclaim its power and status in the world, and to recreate its economic ties with former Commonwealth countries.

In brief, the UK had become "a country that is deluding itself into its supposed rank in the world", as Florentin Collomp from *Le Figaro* stressed. The country is dreaming of its imperial past but with no real facts to back this vision. "Playing Asterix[1] against the whole world is not a smart idea at the moment", Sonia Stolper said. And Brexit will not provide them with any magic potion.

How did that happen? Why has one of the most important nations in the world, part of a relatively stable economic and political union, decided to leave the EU? The answer lies in the deep Euroscepticism that has fostered over the years in the British public sphere.

"What did the UK do to improve the EU?"

In France, even though Frexit has become a growing option in the past few years, it has always been put out of the national debate by the largest part of the traditional French parties and media. On the contrary, in the UK, the European Union has always represented the perfect scapegoat for every single national issue.

"In France, we have considered that Brexit was an accident coming out of nowhere", Alexandre Counis from *Les Échos* said. "But the UK has never been a driving force of the EU, and never has the population stopped being Eurosceptic. It is a country that has always been among the most critical toward the EU and that has always fought the project from the inside".

Daniel Desesquelle got the same feeling once, at the British embassy in Paris: "I asked the ambassador: 'What did the UK do to improve the EU?' He admitted at some point their lack of commitment".

Since Brexit, this general belief has become even stronger. Tabloids picture the EU as trying to scam the UK, while France and his president Emmanuel Macron are described as hard negotiators willing to weaken them. "I am always stunned when UK media say 'May is going to Europe'", Florentin Collomp said. "Their insularity makes them consider Brexit negotiations as a constant balance of power in a zero-sum game".

Most of my interviewees thought the same: the islander mind of the United Kingdom is a factor that played out for the Leave vote. Sonia Stolper said: "As a foreign correspondent, I consider this vote as a slap in our face and over what we symbolise: the foreigner and the EU". Quentin Dickinson added: "When the last time you had been militarily invaded was back in 1066, one can forgive you of having an islander mind".

A self-centred vision of Brexit

UK politicians and media outlets are at least now realising that opening their mind to the other side of the Channel is just as important. "Before Brexit, it was impossible to reach politicians", Sonia Stolper said. "Once I asked David Cameron for an interview. He was not even PM at the time, but I got the following reply: 'Your readership does not vote for us.' Actually, very few UK politicians read the foreign press".

Since Brexit, politicians have opened their door to foreign journalists as they have seen the opportunity to communicate to European leaders and audience. But for years, UK politicians have proved to be uninterested in the European context. Their lack of sensibility and knowledge is another layer to be added to the pile of explainable factors that caused Brexit.

Brexit, Trump, Gilets Jaunes: a Western media failure?

For journalists, Brexit has also been a moment of introspection: how come the progressive and liberal image of the EU has been pushed away by more than 17m people? Of course, talking of a 'post-truth era'[2] as Katharine Viner explained after the vote is central to the analysis. But what about the disconnection between the traditional news media and the Eurosceptic population?

"I did not stay in an ivory tower in London before Brexit and I covered several pro-Brexit areas", Florentin Collomp said. "But it is true that we did not see it coming". The divide had become important, between a population feeling left out by globalisation and the European media outlets –traditionally pro-EU. "There is a media issue here: during the Brexit vote, the media saw what they wanted to see. This vote was hard to analyse, as it was a deep popular feeling and had nothing to do with economic rationality", Alexandre Counis said.

And as the vote became official, the fault was imposed on the Leave voters, who did not vote adequately and must have either felt bad or ignorant; in France, many articles focused on repentant Leave voters ashamed of their vote while others mentioned the sudden peak in Google searches regarding the question "What is the EU" – a story that got debunked[3].

At the end of 2018, the calls for a second referendum sounded the same: "What annoys me is that people deny an obvious fact, the neat victory of the Leave vote", Alexandre Counis said. "It is not arguable to bring a second referendum on the table, and it is not the role of the media to do so."

Finally, Brexit needs to make us think about what this phenomenon meant.

"More widely, we can see that what we called Brexit in the UK, we call it now Gilets Jaunes in France", Quentin Dickinson said. Indeed, Brexit was the first step. Trump's election followed a few months later. In Italy, the far-right movement Lega took power with the populist Five-Star movement in mid-2018; and at the end of the year the Gilets Jaunes movement was taking place in France.

If each phenomenon had its national specificities, all of them showed one thing – that a large part of the citizenry was not willing to listen to traditional politicians and media anymore. All these events were the expression of a deep anger coming from people and areas that have been overlooked for years.

More interestingly, as I write in December 2018, the Gilets Jaunes are reshaping the political debate in France as they ask for more democratic representation[4]. But the trend is moving global. Voters that have felt left out of the debate for years are now willing to be part of it. All traditional Western politicians as well as journalists have to be aware of this new setting; if they do not do so, they may well be speaking in their own bubble.

Notes

1. The French comic character from Brittany. With the villagers of his tiny village, he resists the powerful Rome of Julius Caesar, thanks to a specific magic potion.
2. Katharine Viner is the editor-in-chief of *The Guardian*. Viner, Katharine (2016) How technology disrupted the truth, 12 July. Available online at https://www.theguardian.com/media/2016/jul/12/how-technology-disrupted-the-truth, accessed on 21 December 2018.
3. McGoogan, Cara (2016) *Were Britons really Googling 'What is the EU?' after voting to leave?*, 27 June. Available online at https://www.telegraph.co.uk/technology/2016/06/27/were-brits-really-googling-what-is-the-eu-after-voting-to-leave/, accessed on 21 December 2018.
4. The movement has brought back in the national debate the idea of the democratic referendum tool when asked by a certain number of citizens ("Référendum d'initiative citoyenne").

References:

McGoogan, Cara (2016) *Were Britons really Googling 'What is the EU?' after voting to leave,* 27 June. Available online at https://www.telegraph.co.uk/technology/2016/06/27/were-brits-really-googling-what-is-the-eu-after-voting-to-leave/, accessed on 21 December 2018.

Viner, Katharine (2016) How technology disrupted the truth, 12 July. Available online at https://www.theguardian.com/media/2016/jul/12/how-technology-disrupted-the-truth, accessed on 21 December 2018.

Interviews

Olivier Berger, Grand reporter for the regional outlet *La Voix du Nord* (Interview made on the 12/12/2018)

Florentin Collomp, Correspondent in London for *Le Figaro* (Interview made on the 11/12/2018)

Alexandre Counis, Correspondent in London for *Les Échos* (Interview made on the 19/12/2018)

Daniel Desesquelle, radio producer at RFI for the program "Carrefour de l'Europe" (Interview made on the 20/12/2018)

Quentin Dickinson, Director of the European Affairs for Radio France (Interview made on the 11/12/2018)

Sonia Stolper, Correspondent in London for *Libération*, (Interview made on the 12/12/2018)

About the contributor

Nathan Gallo is a French freelance journalist and a student specialized in media history and media studies. After finishing his two-year thesis on the French media discourse over the independency of the French press in the 1930s (first class honours), Nathan is now studying for an Erasmus Mundus Master's degree in Media studies. In 2017, at the Aarhus University (Denmark), he produced an academic article about Emmanuel Macron's PR strategy and how it was efficient in Anglo-Saxon media outlets (first class honours, not published). He is now doing his final year at City, University of London in data journalism and financial journalism. He also works for French media outlets specialized in football (*So Foot*). Contact details: nathan.gallo@hotmail.com

Chapter 12

Who are the 'nutters' now?

As a Danish correspondent Mette Rodgers has always been warmly welcomed by British Eurosceptics as a kindred soul, she says. Euroscepticism in Denmark, however, is not what they have made it out to be

A year after the 2010 election landed David Cameron in Downing Street – albeit with the help of the Liberal Democrats – I wrote a series of articles for my Danish newspaper exploring the DNA of the Tory party. My editors and readers were fascinated with this party, which had been out in the cold for 13 years. What were they all about now? And what about that thing they had with 'Europe', which had caused former Prime Minister John Major so much trouble? Where were those 'bastards' now? Had they moved on?

The questions were many and a long list of interviews with people from all parts of the party were planned, including with members of fringe groups such as The Bruges Group, The Freedom Association and The Monday Club – some harder to arrange than others as it had to be done by good old-fashioned letter writing.

All, however, were more than happy to talk to me, because – as I would find out – Denmark was considered a kindred spirit; especially by the Eurosceptics. And – I soon realised – that thing about 'Europe' had by no means gone away.

If the UK didn't leave the European Union, it would eventually end up as a 'province of Greater Germany', Bill Cash – the veteran Eurosceptic and one of the original Maastricht rebels – told me in an interview. A view often repeated at meetings on the Conservative right.

"You Danes don't like the EU either", were usually one of the first comments, when I was warmly welcomed. Followed by "You said no to the Maastricht treaty in a referendum, but then you were told that you got it all wrong and had to vote again until you got the right answer".

In fact, this Danish experience was one of the prime examples for the Tory right of the undemocratic nature of 'Europe'. It was one of the main reasons why the UK would have to leave the EU altogether, I was told – although at the time of these interviews in 2011, even the Conservative Eurosceptics themselves were not convinced that it would ever happen.

Not only did the Conservative Party have to share power with the most pro-European party in the country, the Liberal Democrats, their own leader was suspected to be one of them.

"Nobody in the Conservative Party are active supporters of the European Union and yet this is the party's official politics. This government is more pro-EU than even the Labour Party was", Simon Richard, chairman of The Freedom Associations, told me.

Life had changed

In the light of these interviews I soon realised that the issue of British membership of the EU had by no means weakened or gone away since the Major years, although it also seemed to me at the time to be the last roll of the dice by an older generation of Conservatives, who had not woken up to the modern way of life, to globalisation, to the huge transnational challenges of the times and the change of the global balance of power.

The supporters of the idea seemed largely to be older men, and the ideas which accompanied the vision of leaving the EU seemed to me at the time as a far-fetched fantasy, which would never gain support in the wider public, even within David Cameron's 'Compassionate Conservatives'.

They were talking about the UK becoming some kind of 'Singapore on Thames' and about redirecting trade from Europe to the rest of the world, in particular the US and the Commonwealth countries.

As proof that the UK could pull this off, frequent references were made to the time of the Empire; to World War II; to the fact that the UK was a permanent member of the UN Security Council and a bridge between Europe and the United States.

I tended to agree with ITV presenter Robert Peston, who in the foreword of his 2017 book *WTF* wrote: "Those who preferred us out were – let's not be coy about it – nutters."

How naïve I was. Only a few years later, these ideas had become part of the mainstream political discourse. It was their system, which so many Brits bought in June 2016. The vision – at least the part about leaving the EU – is in the process of becoming reality, and as Peston admitted in the next paragraph: "We " – the pro-europeans – "are the nutters now".

'They will join us'

Covering the journey the UK took from when David Cameron in January 2013 promised the nation an in/out referendum on its membership of the EU up until the mess of the negotiations today, I often met the belief among Eurosceptics that "if we leave, Denmark will be the first to join us".

I can see why they might have got that impression. After all the Danes did deliver a no vote in three out of seven referenda since we joined along with the UK in 1973.

The most dramatic referendum result was the no vote in 1992, when asked to accept the Maastricht treaty – the vote often mentioned by British Eurosceptics because it was overturned in a second referendum the next year. Or as former foreign minister Boris Johnson put it in a recent article in the *Daily Telegraph*: "It was the heroic population of Denmark that on that magnificent day in June 1992 stuck two fingers up to the elites of Europe and voted down the Maastricht treaty – and though that revolt was eventually crushed by the European establishment (as indeed, note, they will try to crush all such revolts), that great *nej* to Maastricht expressed something about the Danish spirit: a genial and happy cussedness and independence."

This sentence, however, illustrates where the British Eurosceptics got it wrong. Firstly, the idea that Denmark was not an independent state due to our membership of the EU was never the way the Danes saw it. Only the far-left and the far-right were warning about 'the United States of Europe' – a fear which has become weaker rather than stronger since the Maastricht vote. One reason being that the cooperation has not in fact moved in that direction, with so many countries sharing the worries of

Denmark – and the UK – of the EU regulating areas, which are better regulated nationally.

Another reason probably being that the fringe parties lacked a vision for Denmark outside the EU. Never did anybody seriously argue in the way the British Eurosceptics do, that there would be some kind of huge economic benefit from leaving.

In Denmark it was always about seeking to prevent the EU from watering down our high environmental standards and welfare provisions – again an argument which has faded as especially the left has become more concerned with transnational dangers, such as climate change and the global nature of the financial system, and seems to have accepted that a country of a little more than five million people will be able to do little to save itself from both dangers if we go it alone.

When talking about the second referendum Boris Johnson and many others blame the 'European establishment' for sending the treaty back to the Danish people in a second vote 'to get the right answer'. Never do they mention that it was in fact the Danish political parties on both sides of the argument – although not including the fringe parties – who got together in the aftermath of the rejection in 1992 and collectively pinned down exactly which areas they believed had triggered a small majority of 50.7 per cent to reject the treaty.

Having come up with four concrete concerns – a so-called national compromise – the Danish government went back to the EU and secured, with the help of John Major's government, a number of legally binding opt-outs. Denmark would for example not take part in the Eeuro and parts of the security and defence cooperation.

The year after, a majority of the Danes decided, that given the opt-outs they now felt that their worries had been addressed and thus voted yes to the treaty. There was no bullying, no crushing, no EU elite, just cross-party cooperation and a willingness from the rest of the EU to be flexible.

Rather than praising this example of working together in the national interest, the Brexiteers of today have twisted the handling of the crisis in 1992 to fit in with the British Eurosceptic narrative of the colonial nature of the EU; the colonial master telling its dominion to obey and bow to its demands. And in this way, they have made the Danish Euroscepticism into something heroic, a revolt, rather than a concrete critique of certain parts of a European treaty.

Danes want to stay

"It's not going to happen", I would always say, when it was suggested to me that Denmark would follow the British example and leave the EU.

It was obvious that I was not believed. And if I was, it was put down to the fact that Denmark was such a small country. The UK on the other hand was big and strong enough to make it on its own. And when Denmark and other EU countries saw how the UK would flourish outside, they would surely want to follow.

In fact, the EU would have collapsed within five to ten years of the UK leaving, Nigel Farage predicted at a meeting in the Foreign Press Association in the summer of 2018.

So far developments are not exactly moving in that direction. On the contrary, the invitation from the Brexiteers to join the exodus have instead had the effect of reminding the Danes – and other Europeans – why we should be part of the EU, despite the parts of it which we do not like.

In fact, support for staying in the EU has become stronger in Denmark since the British Brexit vote. According to the Eurobarometer in October 2018 77 per cent of Danes would vote to remain in the EU if asked in a referendum then. Only 14 per cent would vote to leave. These numbers are up from 64 per cent for staying and 27 per cent for leaving a year before. The pattern is the same in the rest of the EU, where 66 per cent would vote to remain and only 17 per cent are willing to follow the UK out of the EU.

So there we are. A continent full of 'nutters' wondering – hoping – that one day, the Brits will be crazy enough to rejoin us in one way or another.

About the contributor

Mette Jørgensen Rodgers has been a correspondent in the UK since 2009, first for the Danish Daily Information and then, since February 2018, for the weekly newspaper Weekendavisen.

Chapter 13

Brexit is just a sideshow. Poland is becoming more important

From behind the iron curtain, the West was perceived a better place. Eventually, this unquestionable sympathy has come to an end, it seems. For many in Poland, 'the West' now means moral nihilism. So does it now mean 'Polexit'? Hanna Liubakova reports

At the passport desk an immigration officer asked to see my student visa. He rattled out the usual questions. Where are you coming from? What course are you studying? Do you have enough funds to pay for your stay? Show me any supporting documentation, madam.

Clack! Clack!

He finally put a date stamp in my passport and said with a smile, "Welcome to the UK." A few months after the 2016 Referendum, it was not the happiest way to be welcomed to the country.

I was born in Belarus, an Eastern European country which is not a member of the EU. If you come from such a country and want to study in Britain, you would most probably pay a much higher fee for your programme, merely because you are an international, non-EU student. Moreover, it costs £348 to apply for a student visa. And do not forget to bring your tuberculosis test results to the UK embassy. Not that you would know it in 'borderless' Europe.

I would be lying if I said that this is exactly what would happen when Britain leaves the EU. Neither side wants to see a return to long queues at checkpoints, customs posts and surveillance cameras at the border. But somehow they can't agree on a way to do that.

I do not care much about Brexit itself. Similarly, I am not in a position to call anyone ignorant simply because they voted for greater self-government for Britain.

What I do care about is truth. Both sides of the political aisle used controversial arguments, eliminating the supremacy of factuality in a debate. This went uglier. Consider, for instance, Ukip's anti-migrant 'Breaking Point' poster with its echoes of extremist propaganda. Britain used to promote its diversity as one of the jewels in the crown of its society. After Brexit, I couldn't help but think whether people would act differently towards me because of my accent.

"In a very fundamental way we, as free people, have freely decided that we want to live in some post-truth world," wrote Tesich in 1992 (Kreitner: 2016). In 2016, few voters could imagine they were making their decisions on the basis of strong facts. The truth simply ceased to matter.

Nothing new, of course, but political lies are on the rise. And this is exactly what I was observing in Poland in late 2018 where I moved after completing my course in Britain.

Will Poland be the new UK?

It was and still is a question being asked by many, including Donald Tusk, European Council president and a former Polish prime minister. He warned that Poland could follow Britain's example and tumble out of the bloc accidentally.

Jaroslaw Kaczynski, the head of the ruling Law and Justice Party and Tusk's political nemesis, dismissed alarmism on 'Polexit' as an opposition 'propaganda' ploy (Rettman: 2018). Polling data ranked Poland among the most pro-EU member states, and Poles were more likely to be fond of Brussels than most other big members of the club.

But, as the fight between Warsaw and Brussels intensified, so did the bitter remarks directed at the EU by senior Polish officials. Andrzej Duda, the Ppresident, lambasted the EU – from which the country has received billions of euros of funds – as an "imaginary community from which we don't gain much" (Moody and Waterfield: 2018). Jaroslaw Gowin, the deputy prime minister, warned if the bloc tried to stop Poland's judicial changes, it would be "the first step towards the auto-destruction of the EU"

(Shotter et al: 2018). Earlier, former Polish foreign minister Witold Waszczykowski claimed the EU was "under Berlin's diktat" (Rankin: 2017).

They did not go further, insulting the European Union by comparing it to Soviets or Nazis, as the former UK Foreign Secretary Boris Johnson (Ross: 2016) and his successor in office, Jeremy Hunt (Rankin: 2018), did. But there was far more on the Polish side.

Law and Justice exploited the same fears of a Muslim invasion, as the arch-Brexiteer Nigel Farage did. During the last regional election campaign in Poland, the ruling party ran an apocalyptic political ad making clear what would happen if the opposition won the local polls (Prawo i Sprawiedliwość: 2018). The footage showed graphic pictures of street violence, while the voiceover said sexual assaults and aggression could happen if Muslim refugees were allowed to enter the country. Even the ideologically pro-PiS Catholic Church utterly condemned the ad.

I remember having much fun watching a video published on Facebook few years ago that showed a British man wearing a balaclava who tried to burn a European Union flag – only to realise it wouldn't light because of EU law on flammable materials.

At 2017's national centenary march through Warsaw, Polish far-right activists were luckier. The All-Polish Youth, a co-organiser of the event, posted a video of an EU flag being set on fire, as some people chanted "away with the European Union". Next to them, the Polish president marched celebrating a century of Polish statehood.

Though extreme nationalism remains a marginal political phenomenon in Poland, Polish nationalists are the only people who openly insist the country should leave the EU. International media considered it alarming when Polish senior politicians joined far-right groups on the independence march.

The Great non-British Bake Off

Cake is very much a national obsession for Brits. And in post-Referendum Britain it became some sort of a national plan on Brexit – thanks to Boris Johnson who famously said the UK could "have our cake and eat it" as it left the European Union. He even described his policy as "pro having it and pro eating it too". With this approach, the British Government might end up neither having its cake nor eating it.

Look at Poland, which is one of the European Union's biggest success stories. Of those post-communist countries that joined the bloc in 2004, none has benefited more from membership than Poland.

First, it is the cash that was used to build hundreds of kilometres of highways and express roads as well as railways, sports facilities, science and technology parks. It is also the citizens: young Poles who travel and study all over Europe. And then they settle wherever they decide, as nearly one million Polish people have made the UK their home.

But from being a poster child of Europe it is becoming its capricious teenager. Since coming to power in 2015, the right-wing Law and Justice party has been weakening democratic checks and balances. The new government moved swiftly to gain control over the Polish judiciary, the Constitutional Tribunal, the country's Civil Service and public media.

The PiS government announced it would not accept any EU-mandated top-down allocation of refugees. While the party has been accused of undermining the rule of law, its leader told the EU to mind its own business. Warsaw's perceived trampling of democratic norms created and continues to create alarm in Brussels. And still, in nominal terms, Poland receives a bigger slice of the EU cake than any other member state.

Europe is fighting back

Threatened with sanctions from Brussels, Poland in late 2018 reversed its purge on the country's Supreme Court. Luckily for Europe, as I write, it still has its king and queen on the chessboard. For the first time ever, the EU has triggered article seven that could lead to Poland being stripped of its voting rights if the other 26 (if the UK has left) countries agree unanimously. But they won't, because Poland will have Hungary's support, and vice versa.

It follows a gradual assault on democracy in Hungary. Brussels failed to stand up to Victor Orban when he attacked free speech, the independence of justice and the country's NGOs that support migration. No wonder Poland studied the Hungarian playbook carefully. Who could have predicted this? Well, in 2011 Kaczynski already announced that "the day will come when we will succeed and we will have Budapest in Warsaw".

Forget about Brexit. The consequences of some EU member states succumbing to authoritarianism would be more significant for the whole Europe. The EU claims that one of its priorities is to promote democracy worldwide. Would it look credible having anti-liberal populists casually dismantling the democratic system inside the house, with absolutely no meaningful consequences? I guess not.

With Brexit and the migrant crisis on the European agenda, it is hard to think how to make democracy great again. But the EU is not merely a union of trade and money; it is also a union of values. Those values – human and civil rights, freedom of speech and tolerance – are under threat. Defending them is crucial – and won't be a piece of cake.

References

Kreitner, Richard (2016) Post-Truth and Its Consequences: What a 25-Year-Old Essay Tells Us About the Current Moment, 30 November. Available online at https://www.thenation.com/article/post-truth-and-its-consequences-what-a-25-year-old-essay-tells-us-about-the-current-moment/, accessed on 21 December 2018.

Moody, Oliver and Waterfield, Bruno (2018) EU is an imaginary community, Polish president tells supporters, 14 September. Available online at https://www.thetimes.co.uk/article/eu-is-an-imaginary-community-polish-president-tells-supporters-hmdsgb8p5, accessed on 21 December 2018.

Prawo i Sprawiedliwość (2018) Wybierz #BezpiecznySamorząd, 17 October. Available online at https://www.youtube.com/watch?v=rMBVLCGkvX0, accessed on 21 December 2018.

Rankin, Jennifer (2017) Poland reacts with fury to re-election of Donald Tusk, 9 March. Available online at https://www.theguardian.com/world/2017/mar/09/donald-tusk-re-elected-as-european-council-president-despite-polish-opposition, accessed on 21 December 2018.

Rankin, Jennifer (2018) Jeremy Hunt rebuked by EU after Soviet prison comparison, 1 October. Available online at https://www.theguardian.com/politics/2018/oct/01/jeremy-hunt-draws-eu-ire-over-soviet-prison-comparison, accessed on 21 December 2018.

Rettman, Andrew (2018) Kaczynski: No question of Polish EU exit, 18 October. Available online at https://euobserver.com/political/143149, accessed on 21 December 2018.

Ross, Tim (2016) Boris Johnson: The EU wants a superstate, just as Hitler did, 15 May. Available online at https://www.telegraph.co.uk/news/2016/05/14/boris-johnson-the-eu-wants-a-superstate-just-as-hitler-did/, accessed on 21 December 2018.

Shotter, James, Huber, Evon and Barker, Alex (2018) Poland warns European Court of Justice to stay out of judicial reforms, 27 August. Available online at https://www.ft.com/content/034718fe-a9dd-11e8-89a1-e5de165fa619, accessed on 21 December 2018.

About the contributor

Hanna Liubakova is an investigative journalist and researcher from Belarus. For the past five years she has been working for the only independent Belarusian TV channel, Belsat. She was a recipient of the prestigious Vaclav Havel Fellowship at Radio Free Europe aimed at supporting journalists from countries lacking media freedom, as well as the Nordic Council international scholarship at Brunel University, London.

Section Three: Old Friends

The grass may not be greener

John Mair

In April 2019 the UK will be out of Europe (maybe). Time for us to seek new trading partners and friends worldwide. Some of those may be old friends in the British Commonwealth – after all, the Empire was the source of British 'greatness' in the 19th and 20th centuries.

Could history repeat itself? Read the views of the correspondents of three old Commonwealth Countries – Australia, India and Bangladesh.

Nick Miller from the *Sydney Morning Herald* sees Brexit as piece of national self-sabotage. Those old bonds will never come back, he says.

Amit Roy is a London-based Indian. He has reported the motherland for decades for the *Telegraph of India*. Having escaped the colonial yoke in 1947, India is now one of the Brics – Brazil, Russia, India, China and Saudi Arabia – the most dynamic economies in the world. Can that trading umbilical cord to the UK be re-tied? Roy heads for our shared passion – cricket – and thinks that even the Geoffrey Boycott of British politics, Prime Minister Theresa May, could find herself out of her crease on that one.

Niaz Alam of the *Dhaka Tribune* in Bangladesh looks to another shared interest – curry and curry houses – for his metaphors. The 2016 Referendum threw up the strange phenomenon of 'Brown Brexiteers' – British Asians who supported Brexit in the hope that fewer Bulgarians would mean more Bangladeshi chefs! It will not. The whole post-Brexit trading situation will be not so much a gentle korma but a complete British stew.

The old friends may still be extant but they have since made new friends in their geographical sphere far away from the UK. They may not prove to be the old/new friends whom Britain needs.

Chapter 14

The view from Down Under: 'What's in it for us?'

Australia has had its fair share of political turbulence in recent years, but many there cannot understand what some see as an act of simple self-sabotage, says Nick Miller

In Liverpool, a month or so after the Brexit Referendum vote, I tried that old foreign correspondent standby: interrogate a taxi driver. "How did you vote?" I asked. "Brexit, no question," he said, emphatically, with a challenge implicit in his voice. "Why?" I replied. He told me he had once picked up a distressed woman from a nightclub, late at night, and she told him she had just been sexually assaulted by a North African immigrant.

After taking a few moments to digest this, I asked the obvious question: "But what's that got to do with Brexit?" He had barely begun answering before he accidentally drove through a red light, triggering a camera flash. This was going to cost him.

For an Australian, getting to understand Brexit has been a process of getting to understand the English. I had a slight advantage on some of my compatriots. I was born in England, though my family moved to seek sun, sand and work after the Winter of Discontent in 1978/79 when I was a child.

I retain enough Englishness (and English relatives) to appreciate the lingering distrust of the continent and its people, the instinctive rejection of the post-war plan for all Europe to join in an ode to joy and brotherhood. Europe, I understood, has always been a market to the British, not a project.

And that's why, when my editors in Australia queried the prospect of Brexit in disbelief, I assured them it was a very real chance.

From Down Under it looked like a pointless act of self-sabotage. Australia is one of the world's biggest fans of trade deals. As a self-aware 'middle power', we know that we prosper through alliances. We have few Empire romances to fall back on (though we have the Commonwealth, more of that later). We instinctively seek to draw ourselves closer to our neighbours, friends and trading partners through deals and forums.

The sight of a country deliberately throwing away a close, mutually beneficial partnership, wilfully damaging its economy and influence on a point of cultural principle, was a surprise.

Fascinating drama

From the start there was an immediate interest from our readers — reflected in the below-the-article arguments and in article click-throughs. I soon found myself writing seemingly endless updates, analysis pieces and weekend news reads on this technical, political spasm on the other side of the world.

In the pre-Trump era Brexit was the international focus for a global trend: the rise of nationalism, the disillusionment with globalism, the fear of 'uncontrolled' migration.

These factors have been playing out in Australia too, though with different timing and emphasis. We managed to make it through the financial crisis more or less unscathed, so the economic triggers for Brexit were alien to us, or at least less relatable. Australian salaries are high and public services pretty robust. But our housing availability/affordability bubble is as bad as Britain's, with similar knock-on effects for quality of life.

Our migration 'crisis' came in 2001, with a surge in the numbers of asylum seekers trying to reach Australia by boat. Our then centrist, populist Prime Minister John Howard seized the moment to proclaim: "We will decide who comes to this country and the circumstances in which they come".

It was a resonant phrase. Like the best political slogans it was impossible to argue with, defending controversial politics with impenetrable rhetoric. When Australians heard the Brexiteer slogan 'Take back control' we immediately recognised what was going on.

David Cameron could have taken a leaf from Howard's playbook. When Howard was confronted with an irresistible push for a referendum in the late 90s (on Australia becoming a republic, which Howard strongly opposed), he responded with a process ingeniously designed to undermine it: first a national convention to agree on a model that was inevitably going to be a compromise nobody liked, then a vote in which half the people who wanted a republic would vote against it because it wasn't the republic they had imagined. Sadly, Howard didn't offer this advice or Cameron didn't seek it.

Reading tea-leaves

So the campaign began. As a foreign correspondent I rarely had to report the daily tennis match. This avoided much of the problem faced by domestic media: the failure of 'he said she said' journalism when confronted with daily exaggerations and concoctions from campaigners, and the rejection of expertise.

Instead, my editors wanted to know what was driving public opinion. Not quite a forecast of the result, but understanding of, whichever way it fell, why it had fallen that way.

My initial theory was that it would shake out much like the 2014 Scottish Referendum. It was to be nationalistic passion and vague promises of future benefits, up against a well-organised steamrolling campaign of warnings about the inevitable costs and risks.

I leaned towards the theory of one YouGov pollster, who told me: "In the ballot box [voters] will give consideration to the wider implications, your pension, your job and your prospects of employment. That's when reality starts to bite and this ephemeral quality of sovereignty and patriotism gets trumped by, quite frankly, 'f--- me, I'm going to lose my job'".

But then I met an insightful Brussels think tank chief, whose depressing logic completely changed my mind.

Fabian Zuleeg told me the above theory was "plausible... but not one I believe in". He asked the simple question: "Who's going to campaign against Brexit?" Business would be reticent, worried about spooking shareholders. Much of the media were scathingly Eurosceptic. Trade unions were never really on board with the EU. Labour was divided.

Cameron was on the nose with voters and had for years (like many of his colleagues) used the EU and immigration as a political punch bag. On the other side were figures like Boris Johnson and Nigel Farage: stump speakers with mass appeal. I'd met Farage. I understood why he was political catnip.

"It's quite frightening," the think tank chief said. "If you look at the general attitudes towards migration (in the UK) it's intensely negative and I think this is going to drive a lot of this agenda."

Australia's view

For an Australian to lecture the UK on political self-harm is, of course, the height of hypocrisy. We've changed prime ministers six times in the last 11 years, only twice as the result of an election, and we're quite likely to do it again in 2019. And if any country is going to sympathise with a nation torn by an endless debate over migration, it's Australia.

Before the Referendum Prime Minister Malcolm Turnbull, though, channelled the mood of much of our country ahead of the Brexit vote: bemused tolerance. "If the British people, in their wisdom, decide to stay in the European Union then we would welcome that," he said a month or so ahead of the vote.

There was self-interest too, Turnbull said. Australian businesses like to base in the UK and take advantage of access to the EU. And Australia as a member of the Five Eyes group, sharing intelligence with the UK, felt from a security point of view "it is an unalloyed plus for Britain to remain in the EU".

Then came the vote. "We respect the wishes of the British people," Turnbull said afterwards. Rather optimistically, he added: "I have no doubt that in due course, the British Government will negotiate a satisfactory departure from the European Union".

Privately, he held a different view. After being deposed, at a private speech in November 2018, Turnbull said what he really thought. Brexit was a "catastrophe", he said – a decision "not even understood by the Government, let alone by the people. It was absolutely uninformed consent".

Nevertheless, a significant faction of conservative Australian politics (including the then High Commissioner in London) threw itself enthusiastically behind Brexit.

Since Brexit our official attitude has been, essentially, "ok, what's in it for us". Most obviously, there's a trade deal. Australia hopes to be the first cab off the rank for a post-Brexit free trade deal. We've a lot of recent experience in getting them done fast.

We're a relatively minor trading partner for the UK (compared with, say, the US), so there's less at stake and the UK can use us as a kind of training ground before it takes on the ruthless brainboxes from Washington DC. And there's the Commonwealth link. Brexiteers imagined Commonwealth ties as a new/old basis for post-Brexit UK's international identity. Australia is happy to play along with this, especially as Brexiteers seem to think the Commonwealth consists entirely of Australia, New Zealand and Canada.

And, finally, it feels like a historical revenge served cold. When the UK joined the EU it triggered a dramatic change in UK-AU trade. We lost a market, and it forced us to refocus on our region. In a way it was a favour: Australia prospered hugely from its growing ties to the developing economies to our north. But some (especially the older, more Anglophile corner of conservative politics) have never forgotten this slight. When Britain comes begging for post-Brexit favours, it will be a sweet moment indeed.

About the contributor

Nick Miller has been the Europe correspondent for the Sydney Morning Herald and The Age, based in London, since 2013.

Chapter 15

It's not all cricket

The British-Indian relationship runs deep, involves millions of people, and is worth billions of pounds – so it has not been an easy story to report, as Amit Roy writes

Reporting Brexit to India can sometimes be fun, as, for example, when the British Prime Minister Theresa May compared herself to the former England batsman Geoffrey Boycott.

Indians enjoyed the cricketing analogy when May told a Downing Street press conference: "Leadership is about making the right decisions, not the easy decisions...you might recall from previous comments I have made about cricket that one of my heroes was always Geoffrey Boycott. And what did you know about Geoffrey Boycott? He stuck to it and got the runs in the end".

Indians realised the analogy was not entirely flattering. Although Boycott accumulated 8,114 runs, with 22 centuries, in 108 Tests between 1964 and 1982, he was also deliberately run out by Ian Botham, a batsman on his own side, in an England-New Zealand match in Christchurch in February 1978 because of the captain's slow and allegedly selfish batting.

Indians realised Brexit was getting a bit serious when May had to move the Diwali party she was planning to host at 10 Downing Street, for some 300 of the movers and shakers of the UK's Indian community across the road to the Foreign Office. The mountains of sweetmeat, an essential part of the Hindu 'Festival of Light', also had to be rearranged in the Foreign Office where Philip May stood in for his absent wife.

What do Indians think of Brexit?

So what do Indians think of Brexit? Firstly, there are the Indians in India – 1.3bn of them who are not entirely convinced of the economic wisdom of Britain leaving the European Union. And then there are the 2.5m people of Indian origin living in the UK who have becoming increasingly uneasy that Brexit appears to be dominated by the right wing of British politics.

Prafulla Mohanty, an artist who arrived in London in 1965, sent me an email out of the blue: "Brexit is making me feel like an immigrant again".

The Bombay-born sculptor, Sir Anish Kapoor, raged at the Referendum result: "I am heartbroken. I hang my head. I feel shame, shame, shame at the xenophobia of this country...I think the three men involved – Michael Gove, Boris Johnson and Nigel Farage – are despicable. And I feel shame, too, at the horrific lack of wisdom, at the criminal abandonment of duty, by David Cameron...he's taken us to an abyss".

It has not been difficult finding Brexit stories with Indian angles.

Virendra Sharma, the Labour MP for Ealing Southall, who has a high proportion of Indians in his constituency, said: "Many of my constituents will now be worse off".

Among leaders of the Indian community, Kartar Lalvani, president of the UK's no 1 vitamins company, Vitabiotics, predicted Brexit would be "very unwise and likely to be disastrous"; while Lord (Karan) Bilimoria of Cobra Beer, argued "the EU is vital for inward investment".

Apurv Bagri, president and CEO of the Metdist Group of companies trading in copper and other non-ferrous metals and also chairman of governors at the London Business School, told me: "I think economically the country will pay a high price; it won't pay it today or tomorrow but over a one to 20-year period. It will change the character of the City of London and its capacity to generate wealth".

The damage for science

The Indian-origin Nobel Laureate and president of the Royal Society, Prof Sir Venkatraman Ramakrishnan, feared leaving the EU would damage British science: "The whole business of European science and collaboration with Europe has been good for everyone in Europe, including Britain, over the last 40 years. It has really led to a flourishing of European science and I would hate that to be disrupted."

Ralf Speth, chief executive of Indian-owned Jaguar Land Rover, warned: "A bad Brexit deal would cost Jaguar Land Rover more than £1.2bn profit each year."

Brexit, however, has led to the spotting of a rare species – British Asians who are hardline Brexiteers, of whom the most high profile is Priti Patel, a former cabinet minister who was picked out by David Cameron for promotion as his 'diaspora champion' but then went against him in the EU Referendum.

She did make at least one good point, which is that when free moment of labour from the European Union ends, applications for visas from Indians to work and live in the UK will not be discriminated against in favour of the nationals of 27 EU member states. Indians certainly will benefit if the cap on Indian doctors and engineers is removed, as the (Pakistani-origin) Home Secretary Sajid Javid has promised.

Although May apologised for her choice of words, she did tell the annual conference of the Confederation of British Industry: "Once we have left the EU...it will no longer be the case that EU nationals, regardless of the skills or experience they have to offer, can jump the queue ahead of engineers from Sydney or software developers from Delhi".

Prospects of an FTA

India is a major economy with which the UK is keen to sign a free trade agreement, but this cannot be concluded until it has formally left the EU. The prospects for such an FTA do not seem very bright since Britain wants to flood India with cheap whisky – not exactly a priority for India – while the Indians want concessions on visas for students and business travellers, which is unlikely to happen while May is Prime Minister.

While reporting Brexit, I remember the advice given to me during my *Daily Mail* days by Sir David English, to my mind the greatest editor Britain has produced. He urged me not to get too bogged down with issues. "Tell your story through people", he said.

So when in doubt always toss in Boris Johnson, whose wife – soon to be ex-wife – is Marina Wheeler, who is the daughter of a Sikh mother, Dip Singh, and the late English journalist, Sir Charles Wheeler.

In writing about Brexit, I have to bear in mind all sorts of personal connections. Boris and I were colleagues during my *Daily Telegraph* days – "we *Telegraph* people must stick together," is his call to arms.

Part of the Brexit story has been the *Daily Mail*'s hardline almost Brextremist stance championed by its recently retired editor, Paul Dacre, and how his policies have been reversed by his successor, Geordie Greig. Actually, I found Paul a sympathetic and intelligent deputy news editor, foreign editor and features editor on the *Mail*, while young Geordie was a colleague when we were on the Andrew Neil-edited *Sunday Times*.

The Indian Government line on Brexit was laid out pretty early on by Narendra Modi on a visit to the UK in November 2015. During a joint press conference with Cameron in the imposing Locarno Room of the Foreign Office, he was asked how he hoped people would vote in the Referendum.

"I believe that the citizens of this country are very intelligent and wise," replied Modi. "I have nothing to say to them, as far as India is concerned".

But then he did go on: "If there is an entry point for us to the European Union, that is the UK and that is Great Britain. And if we have economic co-operation with any country, then the largest economic co-operation is with the UK. Yes, we are going to other European Union countries as well, but we will continue to consider the UK as our entry point into the European Union, as far as possible".

The value of bilateralism

Bilateral relations between India, which is set to replace the UK as the world's fifth biggest economy based on GDP in 2019, and the UK are important. Over the last ten years or so, India has become the fourth largest investor in the UK. Many of the Indian companies had come to the UK, with its population now of 67m, with the ambition of expanding into the 500m-strong EU market.

I have done stories based on comments from Anuj Chande, head of the South Asia Group for Grant Thornton UK, the accounting and consulting firm.

Referring to a report, *India meets Britain Tracker: The latest trends on Indian investment in the UK 2018*, he said: "Our report identifies there are around 800 Indian companies based here and the combined turnover is a staggering £46.4bn – a remarkable contribution to the UK economy. In total these employ nearly 104,932 people".

Chande added: "Whilst it is still too early to predict what impact Brexit will have on the UK's attractiveness as an investment destination for Indian companies, the many advantages the UK can offer are not set to disappear.

"Yet the UK must not take the presence of Indian companies for granted...the UK must ensure that, as it attends to its relationship with the wider world post Brexit, it protects and promotes the factors that make it such an attractive destination for Indian investment".

The Brexit story is set to run for a while yet. What is always appreciated by the copy taster is a touch of masala.

About the contributor

Amit Roy is Europe correspondent of *The Telegraph* of India and editor at large at *Eastern Eye*, a British Asian weekly newspaper.

Chapter 16

Takeaway Brexit Masala – a Bangladeshi perspective

When they talk about us we think they usually mean themselves, says Niaz Alam

Late November 2018. A blustery evening in central London. The Foreign Press Association Media awards and British Curry Awards are taking place at the same time in Mayfair and Battersea respectively.

Both sumptuous annual ceremonies regularly host senior politicians speaking for their supper. Only one topic is on their lips tonight, of course. Two and a half years after the Referendum, no-one is still quite certain what will happen next with Brexit.

I confess to a tinge of patriotism that the event with fewer journalists and more Bangladeshis present, gets closer to reflecting public opinion outside the Westminster bubble.

"Curry brings people together", pronounces Russell Brand to a Bangladeshi camera crew. A trite platitude by the stand-up's standards, but who can argue with a new parent out on a date night, when the hosts have sat Nigel Farage and Vince Cable together at the same table.

Neither the activist comedian, ardent leaver or avuncular Europhile, were the main attraction or speaker amid a sea of restaurateurs. But the trio's cameo roles make Brand's point.

With the political class in disarray and opinion-mongers trapped in an endless Escher loop of Brexit debate, much of the British public would rather change the subject and find something less divisive. In the search for a glue, curry will do.

Curry and nostalgia please

Most journalists, especially foreign correspondents know the risks of relying on outdated stereotypes to explain issues. Tempting as it is to 'print the legend,' it's usually best avoided.

As people tied together by empire and the Commonwealth for centuries, you can easily find folk in both Bangladesh and the UK who know a lot about each other's countries. This being the 21st century, in both places you will hear millennials talking more about *Game of Thrones* than cricket. But sooner rather than later, someone will acknowledge "plenty of British people like curry, Indian restaurants in the UK multiplied rapidly after WWII, and many if not most of these 'Indians' are run by people of Bangladeshi heritage." This is one trope from which there is no escape.

It is apt then that Enam Ali, the founder of the British Curry Awards, is a Bangladeshi-born entrepreneur who came to Britain as a teenager from Sylhet in 1974. Bangladeshis played a pivotal part in making 'going out for a curry' part of Britain's collective consciousness during the now far-off, pre-Single European Act days of 'flock paper tandoori' Indian restaurants.

Large swathes of Britain it seems, recall growing up with a Chinese-run chip shop and Sylheti-staffed Indian curry house as their only available takeaway choices.

Nostalgia is part of the brand. Long before 2001 when Robin Cook, the late Foreign Secretary dubbed 'chicken tikka masala' as Britain's national dish, the Bangladeshi-run curry house was already both a High Street staple and victim of its own success. More profits were now made selling ingredients and ready meals, while choice and competition within the restaurant sector exploded.

It was against this background that the leader of the Bangladesh Caterers Association threw his support behind the Leave EU campaign in the belief Brexit would make it easier to import cheap chefs from South Asia.

Libertarians and rose-tinted fans of Empire alike boosted this prospect in right-wing circles as a dividend of Britain 'freeing' itself from Europe and 'opening the UK up to the world'.

It is a testament of sorts to integration that calls by Boris Johnson and Priti Patel to 'Save Our Curry Houses,' resonated far and wide as part of the populist call to vote Brexit. Murad Qureshi, a three-time elected Labour member of the London Assembly has observed drily that British Bangladeshis know all about referendums. (Sylhet, the north eastern city and district that is ancestral home for a majority of UK Bangladeshis was the only part of British India to hold a plebiscite in 1947 to actively vote to change states during Partition. Less than 24 years later, the same people were voting to leave Pakistan.)

Despite being on the winning side the caterers' goal, just like other Brexit promises, looks less than likely to be delivered.

Not surprising really. A desire to 'take back control' of immigration from European nations was hardly likely to encourage more immigration of low-paid Asian migrants. Being part of a community used to enduring and resisting racism in the UK, and which largely voted to remain, the caterers should have known better. At the British Curry Awards, no-one is surprised when Nigel Farage gets booed.

Below the radar

Spring 2014. Late Friday evening in a humid and warm Dhaka. Out of the blue, I am interviewing Bernard-Henri Lévy in his hotel after a long day.

The celebrated French public intellectual is on a flying visit to launch a Bangla translation of his very first book, *Bangla-Desh, Nationalisme dans la révolution*, about the time he answered the late Andre Malraux's call for an international brigade to support Bangladeshi freedom fighters in 1971 and ended up after the war working a while as a civil servant for the Bangladesh Ministry of Economy and Planning.

Responding to a question about why his oldest book had not been translated wider or earlier, he laments, "It says a lot about the way the world looks at Bangladesh. Not as a key problem. Not as the beginning of something." This strikes a chord. Bangladeshis are used to being overlooked. Global interest in most things Bangladesh tailed off sharply after its early years of independence.

Few outsiders pay attention as it holds its 2018 General Election at the end of December. The eighth most populous country in the world, barely bigger than England but home to more people than Russia, Norway and New Zealand combined, gets less international press than the Golden Globes.

If the legacy of history and global footprint of British culture means the UK as a nation can't help but to punch above its weight in the world, Bangladesh distinctly flies below the radar.

Geography and history offer some reasons why. Most of Bangladesh's history is tied up within that of India, Pakistan and the East India Company. Bangladesh's 160m people are less than a tenth of the population of the South Asian sub-continent. And the same dynamic applies within the UK. At around 450,000 strong, almost half of whom live in London, the British Bangladeshi community is thriving. But likely to be viewed by others (and often themselves) as part of the much larger numbers (c.3m) for the partially overlapping British Asian and British Muslim communities.

In 2015, three British Bangladeshi women – Tulip Rizwana Siddiq, Rushanara Ali and Rupa Huq – from very different family backgrounds were elected as MPs for three very different London constituencies. But three teenage 'jihadi brides' from Bethnal Green got more headlines. "They don't know about us" is a perennial complaint among Bangladeshis abroad.

Stranger than fiction

"Make America Great Again" hats sold at Donald Trump's inauguration were made in China, Vietnam and Bangladesh – *Daily Mirror*, 21 January 2017.

"T-shirts sold at Marine Le Pen rally found to be made in Bangladesh," – *Independent*, 3 May 2017.

Barking, c.2012 Olympics. I wander into a brand-new Italian coffee shop near the station. The décor and modishly dressed owner exude Milano style and confidence. It takes a full ten minutes until he answers a phone in Bengali, before I realise he is Bangladeshi. Some months later, I read about several thousand Bangladeshis with Italian passports joining their more numerous white counterparts in moving to Britain. From the southern European perspective, East London is still a land of opportunity. Just the type of news to stir both pride and fear in many a Brexiteers heart.

Changing stereotypes

Ask a stranger to name a famous Bangladeshi today and one name rules them all.

From *Great British Bake Off* to national treasure in three short years, Nadiya Hussain is deservedly the most famous Bangladeshi in Britain. A natural television presenter, her personal story is challenging all sorts of stereotypes. (Though, not of course our link to food.)

As for Bangladesh, most British people know better than to ask "is that near India" but not so much the trifecta of floods, climate change and disaster won't come up. Cheap clothes, before and increasingly after the Rana Plaza disaster, challenge for the top of the list. In 2018, Bangladeshi manufacturers reportedly overtook China with a 27 per cent market share of denim sales to the EU.

The ethnic cleansing of Rohingya from Myanmar brings new types of attention, A BBC military soap opera *Our Girl*, even used the fact of Bangladesh hosting refugees to provide a backdrop for several episodes. (Artistic licence is one thing, but the fictional British Army deployment would get a lot more attention if it happened in real life.)

With more than 7 per cent GDP growth and rising, and the 50th anniversary of its independence (and the *Concert for Bangladesh*) just two years away, Bangladesh's profile is destined to rise.

Yet a cultural cringe remains. The Bangladesh government, unlike Haiti's, did not publicly protest revelations by *The Times* in 2018 that Oxfam had covered up sexual abuse several years earlier by its aid workers in Haiti, and had helped the most senior staff member involved move on to a lucrative NGO post in Bangladesh.

An imbalance of power is the norm. From gentrification in East London to tackling climate change, Bangladeshi voices can struggle for attention, even when they have a lot to say.

When they talk about us, we think they usually mean themselves.

About the contributor

Niaz Alam is London bureau chief of the *Dhaka Tribune* and a member of its editorial board. A qualified solicitor, he has worked on ethical business and responsible investment issues since 1992. He sat on the board of the London Pensions Fund Authority between 2001-2010 and is a former vice-chair of War on Want. He is currently honorary secretary of the Foreign Press Association in London.

John Mair, Neil Fowler (Editors)

Do They Mean Us?

The Foreign Correspondents' View of Brexit

Written by a range of distinguished foreign journalists, the book explores the spectrum of foreign responses to Brexit, the negotiations, and the outcomes for the UK and its partners.

Alex De Ruyter, David Bailey, John Mair (Editors)

Keeping the Wheels on the Road

UK Auto Post Brexit

With just-in-time and huge logistics issues, this book, written by world automotive experts, delves into the outcomes that can be expected post-Brexit and explores the responses that are required.

John Mair, Neil Fowler (Editors)

The Case for Brexit

Written by some of the most prominent Brexiteers, including Patrick Minford and John Mills, this book argues the case for Brexit at the macro and micro level.

John Mair, Paul Davies

Will the Tory Party Ever Be the Same?

With the Tory Party in turmoil, is this an historic moment for the Tory Party? Leading Tories, with contributions promised from Michael Heseltine, distinguished historians, including Richard Gaunt of Nottingham University, and renowned commentators will provide insights into the likely outcomes.

Bite-Sized Public Affairs Books are designed to provide insights and stimulating ideas that affect us all in, for example, journalism, social policy, education, government and politics.

They are deliberately short, easy to read, and authoritative books written by people who are either on the front line or who are informed observers. They are designed to stimulate discussion, thought and innovation in all areas of public affairs. They are all firmly based on personal experience and direct involvement and engagement.

The most successful people all share an ability to focus on what really matters, keeping things simple and understandable. When we are faced with a new challenge most of us need quick guidance on what matters most, from people who have been there before and who can show us where to start. As Stephen Covey famously said, "The main thing is to keep the main thing, the main thing."

But what exactly is the main thing?

Bite-Sized books were conceived to help answer precisely that question crisply and quickly and, of course, be engaging to read, written by people who are experienced and successful in their field.

The brief? Distil the 'main things' into a book that can be read by an intelligent non-expert comfortably in around 60 minutes. Make sure the book enables the reader with specific tools, ideas and plenty of examples drawn from real life. Be a virtual mentor.

We have avoided jargon – or explained it where we have used it as a shorthand – and made few assumptions about the reader, except that they are literate and numerate, involved in understanding social policy, and that they can adapt and use what we suggest to suit their own, individual purposes. Most of all the books are focused on understanding and exploiting the changes that we witness every day but which come at us in what seems an incoherent stream.

They can be read straight through at one easy sitting and then referred to as necessary – a trusted repository of hard won experience.

Bite-Sized Books Catalogue

Business Books

Maiqi Ma
> Win with China
>> Acclimatisation for Mutual Success Doing Business with China

Elena Mihajloska
> Bridging the Virtual Gap
>> Building Unity and Trust in Remote Teams

Rob Morley
> Agile in Business
>> A Guide for Company Leadership

Gillian Perry
> Managing the People Side of Change
>> Ten Short Steps to Success in IT Outsourcing

Saibal Sen
> Next Generation Service Management
>> An Analytics Driven Approach

Don Sharp
> Nothing Happens Until You Sell Something
>> A Personal View of Selling Techniques

Christopher Hosford
> Great Business Meetings! Greater Business Results
>> Transforming Boring Time-Wasters into Dynamic Productivity Engines

Lifestyle Books

Anna Corthout
> Alive Again
>> My Journey to Recovery

Phil Davies
> Don't Worry Be Happy
>> A Personal Journey

Phil Davies
> Feel the Fear and Pack Anyway
>> Around the World in 284 Days

Stuart Haining
> My Other Car is an Aston
>> A Practical Guide to Ownership and Other Excuses to Quit Work and Start a Business

Bill Heine
  Cancer – Living Behind Enemy Lines Without a Map
Regina Kerschbaumer
  Yoga Coffee and a Glass of Wine
      A Yoga Journey
Gillian Perry
  Capturing the Celestial Lights
      A Practical Guide to Imagining the Northern Lights
Arthur Worrell
  A Grandfather's Story
      Arthur Worrell's War

Public Affairs Books

Eben Black
  Lies Lunch and Lobbying
      PR, Public Affairs and Political Engagement – A Guide
John Mair and Richard Keeble (Editors)
  Investigative Journalism Today:
      Speaking Truth to Power
John Mair, Richard Keeble and Farrukh Dhondy (Editors)
  V.S Naipaul:
      The legacy
Christian Wolmar
  Wolmar for London
      Creating a Grassroots Campaign in a Digital Age
John Mair and Neil Fowler (Editors)
  Do They Mean Us – Brexit Book 1
      The Foreign Correspondents' View of the British Brexit

Fiction

Paul Davies
  The Ways We Live Now
      Civil Service Corruption, Wilful Blindness, Commercial Fraud, and Personal Greed – a Novel of Our Times
Paul Davies
  Coming To
      A Novel of Self-Realisation

Children's Books

Chris Reeve – illustrations by Mike Tingle
> The Dictionary Boy
>> A Salutary Tale

Fredrik Payedar
> The Spirit of Chaos
>> It Begins

19819049R00066

Printed in Great Britain
by Amazon